THE
DRAGONS' DEN
GUIDE TO
INVESTOR-READY
BUSINESS
PLANS

THE
DRAGONS' DEN
GUIDE TO
INVESTOR-READY
BUSINESS
PLANS

THE PRODUCERS OF CBC's DRAGONS' DEN with JOHN VYGE

WILEY

John Wiley & Sons Canada, Ltd.

Library and Archives Canada Cataloguing in Publication Data

The Dragons' Den guide to investor-ready business plans / The Producers of CBC's Dragons' Den, John Vyge.
Includes index.
Issued also in electronic format.
ISBN 978-1-118-29879-4
    1. Business planning. 2. Small business--Planning.
3. Dragons' Den (Television program). I. Vyge, John, 1966-
HD30.28.D73 2012   658.4'012   C2012-903031-7
978-11118-31384-8 (ebk); 978-1-118-31383-1 (ebk); 978-1-118-31382-4 (ebk)

Production Credits
Typesetting: Laserwords
Printer: Dickinson

Editorial Credits
Executive editor: Don Loney
Managing editor: Alison Maclean
Production editor:
    Jeremy Hanson-Finger

Partner Credits
Sony Pictures Television:
Lindsay Pearl
    Director of Consumer Product
    Licensing
Lisa O' Connell
    Product & Brand Manager of
    Consumer Product Licensing

CBC Dragons' Den:
Karen Bower
Dianne Buckner
Molly Duignan
Sandra Kleinfeld
Keri Snider
Marc Thompson
Tracie Tighe

John Wiley & Sons Canada, Ltd.
6045 Freemont Blvd.
Mississauga, Ontario
L5R 4J3

Printed in United States of America

1 2 3 4 5 DP 16 15 14 13 12

SONY
PICTURES
TELEVISION

Contents

FOREWORD
By Dianne Buckner

If you've ever thought "preparation" was a dull word, consider that for the hundreds of hopeful entrepreneurs who come to pitch for investment on CBC Television's hit show *Dragons' Den,* preparation is what makes the difference between thrilling success and a big disappointment.

Those who leave the Den triumphant have thought ahead of time about what probing questions the Dragons may ask and have prepared irresistible pitches that outline how they'll help make our five fire-breathing capitalists even richer. They're on their way to the supreme satisfaction that comes from building a business with a strong partner. As for those who did *not* arrive with a business plan and a well-developed presentation—well, if you've seen the show, you know well just how uncomfortable those Dragon flames can be!

The Dragons' Den Guide to Investor-Ready Business Plans will prepare you not only to pitch to Dragons, but also to win over any type of investor. And as the old adage goes, you need money to make money.

Many entrepreneurs go to their bank in the hopes of securing the necessary funds to start up their new company. But the reality is that Canada's big banks rarely do that type of lending. They need to protect their depositors' money with more secure types of investments, and most people starting businesses are not in a position to guarantee their future cash flow. You can try, but that will also take preparation—which this guide will also help with.

It's worth your time to investigate whether you qualify for government programs aimed at boosting entrepreneurship, and in turn, Canada's economy. There are a variety of loans and grants available. They also require business plans (and the patience for highly detailed application forms and interviews).

Then there are private investors, people or organizations with money to put into promising ventures that will give them a solid return. Where can the entrepreneur find them? How should potential investors be courted? What do they need to hear in order for them to hand over their dollars, and will you be able to speak their lingo? If you have a solid business concept, then you're ready to take the next step and secure financing. The book in your hands will explain how that can be done.

(If you're still trying to come up with a money-making venture, refer to John's previous Dragons' Den book, *The Dragons' Den Guide to Assessing Your Business Concept*!)

Consider the story of Catherine Langin and her pitch to turn her father's invention, the Miner's Lunch Box, into a thriving business. Or the efforts made by wife-and-husband team Noémie Desrochers and Vincent Purino with their stylish Aquaovo water purification systems. *The Dragons' Den Guide to Investor-Ready Business Plans* explains how they prepared, and as a result, scored deals with the Dragons.

Or perhaps you'd like to know what can be learned from Coco Chanel's business experience, or that of the founders of Shoppers Drug Mart? John Vyge doesn't limit himself to the lessons from the Den—there's fabulous business lore on every page.

And best of all, this book will allow you to analyze your own business through easy-to-complete quizzes and questions.

In the end, preparation is not-at-all dull. It's an engrossing, fascinating process that leads to success.

Good luck in your quest to bring inspired investors on board!

PART I

THE INVESTOR-COURTING PROCESS

Court investors who have a history of investing in your type of business concept by proving to them that your business concept will work.

CHAPTER 1

THE INVESTOR-COURTING PROCESS

"I'm trying to decide as I'm listening to you guys whether I'm falling in love with your energy and enthusiasm and business savvy for your age, or if I'm falling in love with the idea."
—Dragon to Pitchers

THE INVESTOR-COURTING PROCESS

Courting is a process that starts long before you actually meet an investor to make a pitch. It begins with an idea you have for a business that you believe is viable. The next stage is building a business model and proving that it works. This takes you to the step of obtaining face time with investors to make your pitch and get a deal that makes sense for your business.

Long before launching her fashion empire in 1909, Coco Chanel learned how to sew in a small town in France in the orphanage where she grew up. Before Frank C. Mars started his confectionery business in 1911, his mom taught him how to hand-dip chocolate at home. When Estée Lauder launched her cosmetics empire in 1946, she was able to draw on the experience she gained watching her uncle produce skin creams in their family kitchen. Harry Rosen worked in a clothing factory, where he learned the art of designing and making clothes, before he launched his men's clothing retail chain in 1954. Michael Dell sold newspaper subscriptions years before he used a $1,000 investment to launch his direct-sales computer company out of his dorm room in 1984. And Sara Blakely of Spanx probably had no idea that the sales skills she learned as a fax machine salesperson would help launch an undergarment company that would lead her to become America's youngest female billionaire. The list of entrepreneurs who have used a skill set and past experience to launch their businesses goes on and on.

But when they launched their operations, most of these individuals didn't achieve success by simply sitting down and writing out a business plan. They got it from their ability to meet the needs of a paying customer using the skills they already had. What enabled these people to prosper was their ability to find a market for a product or service that they had built. They developed their skills first, and a sound business plan followed.

Once you prove your business concept, it is time to put a strategy in place to sustain your competitive advantage over the long haul. You have to assume that if your business becomes profitable, somebody somewhere is going to enter your space and compete for market share. Your business plan must have a long-term strategy and address assumptions about facing competitors. Oh, and while you're at it, make sure it's **investor ready**, just in case you need capital to grow.

When Scott Sigvaldason, owner of Cavena Nuda, visited the Dragons' Den with his rice substitute, he had a concept that was more than investor ready. He had $1.5 million in sales the previous year from selling his product as animal feed, but now wanted to sell it as a food product to restaurant chefs across the country. Convincing the Dragons to invest was easier said than done. Fortunately, one Dragon with deep restaurant experience was aware that the price of rice worldwide had gone through the roof, so he decided to seed the company with $250,000 of his own cash.

CAVENA NUDA

Pitcher: Scott Sigvaldason, Season 4, Episode 3

"What we're here pitching you today is a brand new food grain that we've branded and marketed as Cavena Nuda. It looks, it cooks, and it tastes like a rice . . . It's healthier. This has got very high beta-glucan fibre. That's what lowers your cholesterol level."
—Pitcher to Dragons

PRODUCT DESCRIPTION

An oat grain substitute for rice.

DRAGONS' DEN BY THE NUMBERS

- **The Ask:** $250,000 for 20% of the business
- **Company Valuation:** $1.25 million
- **The Deal:** $250,000 for 50% of the business
- **106:** The age of Scott's farm
- **$1,500,000:** Sales last year when Scott packaged his product as animal feed
- **40:** The number of years of restaurant experience that one Dragon brought to the deal

Scott Sigvaldason of Cavena Nuda pitching his rice substitute to the Dragons.

THE WARM-UP: INVESTOR-COURTING PROCESS DEFINED

This book is about making sure that you have a fundable business concept. You can create a properly formatted business plan for just about any business idea you can come up with. But the business-planning process will do nothing to enhance a weak business concept. That's why this book, and its companion, *The Dragons' Den Guide to Assessing Your Business Concept*, go hand in hand to help you focus on first proving your concept, and then creating your business plan. In fact, if you have a proven business concept with customers and the right connections, you might just get funded without a business plan. But don't count on it.

Business plans are a critical due diligence tool that most investors request at some point during the investor-courting process.

The **investor-courting process** is a fundraising process that brings entrepreneurs and investors together to achieve their shared goals of return on investment. The purpose of the investor-courting process is to match entrepreneurs who have fundable business concepts with investors who have funds, who can provide guidance, and who ultimately profit from the relationship. The following are two areas of the investor-courting process that are important to understand:

- **Milestone:** An achievement in the development of your business that the investor will use to measure your performance.
- **Stages of Investment:** A growth stage of your business that will attract different kinds of investors at different times.

Milestones: What Investors Expect

Make no mistake about it, investor capital is provided so that you can achieve business milestones, not so that you can reach the next round of funding. While investor capital can certainly be provided as a precursor to future funding rounds, don't lose sight of what really matters: revenue, profitability, and satisfied customers. Because if you fail to achieve those, you won't need an angel investor anymore—you'll need a white knight to save your business from the abyss!

The initial excitement of a fledgling business concept will quickly disappear if you don't turn your concept into a real business fast. Some key milestones that investors look for—and often help entrepreneurs achieve—are:

- **building a working prototype**
- **acquiring intellectual property**, such as patents
- **conducting a successful beta (or pilot) test** with actual customers
- **achieving sales tractions** in the form of a predictable level of sales coming in each month, quarter, or year
- **achieving commercial viability** by selling your products and/or services in sufficient volume to meet the return on investment (ROI) objectives of the stakeholders in your business
- **achieving profitability** beyond your personal salary

Stages of Investment: When Investors Invest

When entrepreneurs start businesses, they often turn first to the bank for capital. But that's not always the best decision, because a bank will require collateral, such as your house, for its loan. Investors can be a lower-risk source of financing for your business if you have a proven business concept. The amount of investment capital you receive, and who you receive it from, will vary with the stage your business is at. Active investors usually focus on businesses that have achieved a level of growth that interests them. For example, some investors are attracted to seed-stage businesses that have yet to prove their business concept. Other investors are attracted to businesses that have proven business concepts and that simply need capital to tap into new markets. Here are the five stages of investment.

STAGES OF INVESTMENT

Seed Stage	Start-up Stage	Early Stage	Expansion Stage	Late Stage
Prove your business concept.	Launch your business.	Generate a critical mass of customers.	Expand to new markets.	Prepare your company for significant growth or an IPO.

Funding Rounds

When you're seeking capital for your business, it's important to understand the language that investors speak so that you don't get steamrolled during negotiations. One term to understand is a **funding round**, which is a layer of investment capital that is provided to your business to get you to a specific milestone in your business. It's called a "round" because there is a start and stop to the amount of funding you receive. But a round has nothing to do with a particular stage of investment. A venture capitalist can provide seed-stage capital, while an angel can provide late-stage capital. Funding rounds go by various names that you should be familiar with, including the following:

- **Seed Round:** The entrepreneur, the entrepreneur's friends, or angel investors put up capital to help the entrepreneur launch the business. It's also possible to get seed capital from government programs, or banks like the Business Development Bank of Canada.
- **Angel Round:** An angel investor (someone who invests his or her own money, as opposed to an institutional investor who may be working with other people's money) provides capital that helps the entrepreneur grow the business or reach a specific milestone. This is a *growth round* of funding.

- **Series Round:** A venture capital firm (investors of other people's money, usually via a fund) helps the entrepreneur grow the business or reach a specific milestone with multiple rounds of funding, named series A, B, C, D, etc. This is also a *growth round* of funding.
- **Mezzanine Round:** So called because this round comes in between series rounds and an initial public offering (IPO), just like the mezzanine floor comes in between the lower and higher floors of a building. This is where a venture capital firm helps the entrepreneur keep his or her business alive until it goes public.
- **IPO Round:** An investment bank takes an entrepreneur's company public and sells shares on the open market in an initial public offering.

Most people reading this book will only ever have the chance to receive the first two (seed or angel) rounds of funding—if they receive funding at all. Obtaining financing from a venture capital firm, or having an IPO, is an unlikely event for most small businesses because of the large scale of the business required for these events, and the scrutiny placed on the businesses that pitch them.

THE INVESTOR-COURTING PROCESS: OVERVIEW

The process of courting an investor is not an exact science. There are no guarantees that you will ever receive funding, but you can increase your odds of success by staying focused on growing your business, and by following this four-stage systematic approach for meeting investors.

1. **The Investor Pipeline:** Build a network of people who can introduce you to active investors who provide capital to fundable business concepts.
2. **Screening:** Investors will pre-screen and screen your business concept, so you should self-screen your idea to make sure that it has certain factors that investors will look for before they write their cheques. Before they agree to dig deeper into your business plan, investors will pre-screen your idea to ensure that it meets their needs. (For example, some investors concentrate on the biotech industry, or they need to see a certain level of sales.)
3. **Valuation and Funding:** Investors will place a value on your business based on various assumptions that they make. You should determine a realistic value for your business in advance, so that you can make educated decisions during negotiations about the amount

of funding you will receive in return for a portion of your business. (See Chapter 4 for an explanation of how to value your company.)

4. **Due Diligence:** Before they write their cheques, investors will perform due diligence on your business to ensure that the projections and financial forecasts you are making are based on sound business operations. So, you should self-audit your business to make sure that you have the financial, legal, and operational systems in place that investors will look for.

DRAGON LORE

Be more diligent about proving your business concept and making it fundable than about fussing over a properly formatted business plan.

Investors screen business ideas for scalability, realistic revenue models, proof of concept, and evidence of a team of entrepreneurs who are passionate about their ideas. Two entrepreneurs who brought all of these elements together, plus contagious enthusiasm, were Ross Lipson and Howard Migdal of GrubCanada.com. And both of them realized early on in their pitch to the Dragons that a pitch is more than just a one-way presentation—investors will engage you with questions early and often.

GRUBCANADA.COM

Pitchers: Ross Lipson and Howard Migdal, Season 4, Episode 9

BUSINESS MODEL

The company runs a website where customers can view the menus for various local restaurants. It makes money by taking a 9% commission on each order they process and send to restaurants, which then fulfill those orders.

PROBLEM

I'm new to the area and I need to place a takeout or delivery order from a restaurant, but I don't know any restaurants that are nearby.

SOLUTION

An online food court where visitors can type in their address and see all the restaurants that deliver to their location. The visitor then places an order online at GrubCanada.com.

GO-TO-MARKET

Will spend $3 to $5 per person on online marketing to acquire each customer.

TEAM

Founders Ross Lipson and Howard Migdal are 22-year-old roommates from Detroit, Michigan, who now live in Toronto. They used their combined skills to put together a scalable business model that was attractive to multiple Dragons.

FINANCIALS

The Ask: $200,000 for 20% equity in the company
Company Valuation: $1,000,000
Current-Year Revenue Projection: $600,000
The Deal: $200,000 for 50% equity in the company, plus 1% of the 9% commission

Pitchers Ross Lipson and Howard Migdal celebrating their deal.

SELF-STUDY WORKSHOP: The Investor-Courting Process

Determine where you are in the investor-courting process. Identify the stage your business is at. Identify major milestones you have already achieved, and set new milestones for your business. Keep in mind that you will delve deeper into some of these topics later on in this book.

1. What is the current **stage of investment** of your business?
   - ❑ Seed Stage
   - ❑ Start-up Stage
   - ❑ Early Stage
   - ❑ Expansion Stage
   - ❑ Late Stage

2. What **major milestones** have you already achieved? For each milestone listed below, elaborate on what you have completed to date and how you would prove that the milestone has been achieved.
   - ❑ Prototype built
   - ❑ Intellectual property acquired
   - ❑ Beta test completed
   - ❑ Sales traction achieved
   - ❑ Commercial viability achieved
   - ❑ Profitability achieved
   - ❑ Other milestones achieved

3. What are your activities over the next **three months, six months**, and **one year** in each of the following milestone categories? Where applicable, elaborate on the amount of funding you will need to reach the milestone, and when the milestone will be reached.
   - ❑ Build a prototype
   - ❑ Acquire intellectual property (patent, trademark, etc.)
   - ❑ Complete beta test
   - ❑ Generate sales traction
   - ❑ Achieve commercial viability

- ❑ Achieve profitability
- ❑ Other

4. What is the current status of your **investor-courting process**?

   a. Who do you have in your **investor pipeline** who could introduce you to an investor?
      - ❑ Haven't started a list
      - ❑ Have started a list (name them)

   b. What have you done to **self-screen** your business concept and validate that it is fundable?
      - ❑ Nothing
      - ❑ Made sales to paying customers
      - ❑ Read and implement the *Dragons' Den Guide to Assessing Your Business Concept*

   c. What do you think is the estimated **value** of your business, and what amount of **funding** will you require?

   d. What **self-auditing/due diligence** have you completed so far to make sure that your financial, operational, and legal systems are ready to be reviewed by investors?
      - ❑ Financial systems
      - ❑ Operational systems
      - ❑ Legal systems
      - ❑ I don't know what these mean (you will review these concepts in Chapter 5)

In this chapter we reviewed the investor mindset and prepared you for the investor-courting process. In the next four chapters, we'll drill down into each of the four key stages of the investor-courting process so you can put your business in the best possible position to get funded.

CHAPTER 2

HOW TO FIND AN INVESTOR

"You can talk ethics and green and baby whales and chickens and all that stuff . . . In the end they want the lowest cost with the path of least resistance. That's what matters to the consumer."

—Dragon to Dragon

INVESTOR-COURTING STAGE #1: The Investor Pipeline

Cold-calling investors is not a good strategy. You should network to try to secure introductions to investors. Make this your number one priority when trying to grow your business. If you need investor capital, look for a combination of investor know-how and financing. Be open to revising your business model to meet the needs of investors and customers.

The process of getting in front of investors can be like being in the lineup outside a popular bar or restaurant. Every once in a while, the chosen few walk right by you to the front of the line, smile at the bouncer or host, and inexplicably get in the door. The problem is that most investors see the investment process as a game of numbers—called **deal flow**—much like a lineup. The more deals they screen, the more likely they are to find one that meets their return on investment needs. And out of the businesses that they do choose to fund, maybe only 10% or 20% of them will actually pan out or lead to a successful "exit." So you become a number in a lineup, subject to pre-screening, screening, and due diligence processes that are put in place to weed you out. Therefore, when another entrepreneur is referred to the investor by a colleague whom the investor trusts, the investor will often let that entrepreneur walk right past you and through the door to make his or her presentation.

You can capitalize on this process (no pun intended) by making it your goal to get **introductions to investors** who can get you past their gatekeepers, instead of standing in line, to meet investors. And if you're lucky enough to meet them, you can make your efforts more successful by being flexible and open to their advice. So start by making every effort to turn your business idea into an investable business concept. Look for people who can introduce you to investors. Then, instead of having to count on results from just one investor, you'll suddenly have connections and introductions to a whole bunch of them. This list of investor introductions becomes your **investor pipeline**.

Once you do get in front of an investor, ensure that you can show your connection to the problem that your product or service solves, and how the investor can personally relate to it. When Hailey Coleman introduced herself to the Dragons, she brought more than just an investable business concept. She showed up with a personal passion for a product that solved her own problem—sore feet after a long night out in stiletto heels.

DAMN HEELS

Pitcher: Hailey Coleman, Season 5, Episode 1

"After one excruciatingly painful post-party walk home, I decided that walking the streets on barefoot was a faux pas that could and needed to be prevented . . . Women are in need of a solution to save them from their beloved damn heels when they're working, partying, travelling, or at events such as weddings. The solution? Sexy, fold-up ballerina flats tucked into an expandable bag to save women from their beloved damn heels. Women can simply slip their [sore] feet or blistered feet into the soft-sided flats, and their beloved stilettos into the cute reusable bag [that the flats come with]."
—Pitcher to Dragons

PRODUCT DESCRIPTION

Fold-up ballerina flats that tuck into an expandable bag.

DRAGONS' DEN BY THE NUMBERS

- **The Ask:** $25,000 for 33% of the business
- **Company Valuation:** $75,758
- **The Deal:** $25,000 in marketing services, plus $25,000 in cash, for a 5% royalty for 20 years
- **700:** The number of units sold to date
- **2:** The number of Dragons who competed against each other for a deal, with the one female Dragon, who has an intimate knowledge of the pain involved with high heels, sealing the deal.

Pitcher Hailey Coleman demonstrating Damn Heels, her fold-up ballet flats that fit in a purse.

THE WARM-UP: THE INVESTOR PIPELINE DEFINED

An **investor pipeline** refers to the number of investors you are introduced to in your attempt to secure capital for your business. The purpose of building an investor pipeline is to plant seeds with multiple investors who may either fund your business themselves or introduce you to other investors. The process of building an investor pipeline involves finding the following:

- **Sources of Funding**
- **Investor Types**
- **Introductions to Investors**

Sources of Funding

In an ideal world, you wouldn't need start-up capital because your prepaid revenue would pay all of your start-up costs. However, unless you perform a personal service with payments made in advance, this scenario rarely happens. That's not to say that you can't start a business with little or no cash, but most businesses usually require some sort of capital, personal or otherwise, to get started and grow.

Whatever your needs, there are multiple ways of finding investment capital for your business. While this list is certainly not exhaustive, it is offered as a starting point for you to build your investor pipeline. Note that the figures provided here are not hard-and-fast rules, but rather general guidelines. Here are indications of the level of investment capital that you might consider seeking from each type of investor.

First $10K	$10K to $25K	$25K to $500K	$500K+
Bootstrap	**Friends and Family**	**Angel Investors**	**Venture Capital**
Put up **your own funds**, borrow capital from a bank, or use capital from the business itself.	Seek outside investment capital from **friends and family** who are willing to share the risk and reward.	Seek outside investment capital from **angel investors** who provide guidance, their own funding, and connections.	Seek outside investment capital from professional **investment firms** that invest other people's money and provide guidance and connections.

If you are fortunate enough to secure capital from an investor, be sure to see that capital as a bridge that will carry you to your next milestone and onto profitable revenue. Don't lose sight of why it is being provided. Unfortunately, this happens all the time when entrepreneurs use financing to upgrade their offices, purchase new computers, and waste new investment capital on ineffective marketing campaigns. Be clear about how you will use any funds you receive, and stay on track with your business plan until you reach your next financial milestone.

You'll notice that using revolving credit cards and mortgaging your house are not on this list of recommended means of raising finance. Many entrepreneurs have certainly gone this route and succeeded, so why not do it too? Because if you don't pay these loans back, you could lose your house, your credit rating, your credibility, and maybe even your family.

Investor Types

Because attracting investment capital is not an easy process, many entrepreneurs jump at the first investor who agrees to write them a cheque. They are so excited about their business idea that they are certain that the first investor they meet is the right one to help them get there, because time is of the essence.

The reality is that entrepreneurs have to pick their investors wisely. They need to choose an investor who can bring something to the table in addition to the funds they are providing. Ultimately, the fundraising process comes down to your ability to meet the right type of investor, which is why you need to seek introductions to multiple investors—not just one. There are generally two types of investors:

- **Financial Investors:** These investors provide capital, introductions to future investors, some negotiation expertise, and little else. They may be angels, venture capital (VC) firms, or friends and family who make a monetary investment in your business in exchange for a 25% to 50% annualized return, and an exit from the business in five to ten years.
- **Strategic Investors:** These investors provide both capital and know-how. But, in exchange for providing industry expertise, industry contacts, and introductions to future investors, they may offer slightly less favourable terms than you might get with a financial investor. They will still be angels, VC firms, or friends and family, but this time they'll bring with them a background in your business sector that can help you reach your goals faster.

Introductions to Investors

Having an "in" with an investor, either through a direct connection, an endorsement, or through networking activities, is a fast track for an entrepreneur who is looking to pitch a fundable business concept. Few investors will accept a pitch from an entrepreneur without one. That's because investors need to trust the teams they invest in, and nothing engenders trust more than a referral from one of their trusted colleagues or advisers. At the same time, if you are already connected to people who make investments in businesses like yours, then by all means go directly to them.

But getting in the door is no guarantee that the funder will open his or her wallet. Investors want to see proven concepts backed by solid teams, and many want to see that other investors have already endorsed your business concept by investing as well. Here is a four-step approach to start building your pipeline:

1. Clearly define the investment opportunity you're presenting using an **elevator pitch** format (such as the one you'll find in Chapter 7).
2. Make contact with **investor referral sources** who know investors, and let them know that you are looking for guidance from active investors for your new business idea.
3. Create a written **executive summary** (using the format in Chapter 9), and make it available to investor referral sources, or investors you are introduced to, who require it as a precursor to listening to your pitch.
4. Be flexible in your approach to fundraising by showing a willingness to break down your total funding requirement into **smaller amounts with different layers of risk** that can be funded by multiple investors.

Investor Referral Sources

You can always ask people you know to invest in your business, but that can lead to soured relationships and a lot of rejection. Once you have an investable business concept, there is nothing more powerful than an introduction to an investor, and that might be a better strategy. The best way to achieve these introductions is to network with people who make repeated contact with investors. Don't just ask your referral sources if they know anyone who can fund your business. Instead, break the ice by asking them if they know any investors who can guide you through the investment process, or who can help by giving you general feedback. Some good places to **seek introductions** to investors who can help you are as follows:

- **Angel Networks:** Groups of independent investors who share resources to screen, perform due diligence, and invest in business ideas. They have applications that you can fill out online, and they give you an opportunity to upload your executive summary.
- **Professional Advisers:** Accountants, business lawyers, insurance agents, and financial advisers who come in contact with high-net-worth investors who may be looking to diversify their investment portfolios.
- **Friends and Family:** Family members and friends who may know high-net-worth individuals who actively invest in business ideas.

- **Pitching Forums:** Open forums where entrepreneurs can pitch their ideas to groups of angel investors. Entrepreneur applications are screened in advance, and only a select few make it to the forums.
- **Business Plan Competitions:** Local competitions that you don't have to win to get capital. Sometimes your pitch might attract an outside investor, or you might meet investors at the event during networking opportunities that the competitions provide.
- **Business Incubators:** Shared business environments where entrepreneurs are provided with coaching, guidance, and sometimes access to investors or loans in exchange for a rental fee or a percentage of equity.

DRAGON LORE

Avoid contacting investors directly without a formal introduction or personal connection to them. The credibility of your pitch is heavily dependent on the way in which the investor hears about your business idea.

Investors make decisions based on numbers. Sometimes the numbers that an entrepreneur brings to the table may, at first glance, be too low to warrant the investor's interest. But there are businesses with successful histories that an investor may be willing to take a hard look at. Active investors look for value in businesses beyond just the initial revenue you have shown them. If you happen to have a brand with a history that just needs a kick-start, a keen investor will put a value on that and give your business a deal. That was the case when the heir to the May Metal Fabricators lunchbox company visited *Dragons' Den*.

MINER'S LUNCHBOX

Pitcher: Catherine Langin, Season 4, Episode 3

BUSINESS MODEL

The company sells aluminum lunch boxes that retail for between $40 and $90.

PROBLEM

If you sit on most lunch boxes, they collapse.

SOLUTION

A riveted aluminum lunch box, called the Miner's Lunch Box, that is so strong you can sit on it.

GO-TO-MARKET

Word-of-mouth advertising leverages the brand equity that Langin's father, Leo May, built. Leo May developed the original product and sold over a million units.

TEAM

Founder Catherine Langin is the heir to her father Leo May's lunch box company.

FINANCIALS

The Ask: $150,000 for 30% equity in the company
Company Valuation: $500,000
Revenue Last Year: Over $100,000
The Deal: $100,000 in cash, plus a $50,000 loan for 20% equity

The Miner's Lunch Box being pitched on *Dragons' Den*.

SELF-STUDY WORKSHOP: Building an Investor Pipeline

Develop a list of people, places, and events that can help you gain introductions to investors. Start with your own sphere of influence, and then dig deeper by scouring the Web and local and regional news to find events where you can network.

1. What is the estimated amount of **investor funding** you will need?
    - ❑ <$10,000
    - ❑ $10,000 to $25,000
    - ❑ $25,000 to $500,000
    - ❑ $500,000+

2. How have you **funded** your business so far?
    - ❑ Bootstrap (self-funded)
    - ❑ Bank
    - ❑ Friends and family
    - ❑ Angel investors
    - ❑ Venture capital

3. What **type of investor** are you looking for?
    - ❑ Financial Investor: Money only
    - ❑ Strategic Investor: Investment capital, know-how, and industry contacts

4. Who will be your largest source of **introductions to investors**?

5. What is your **60-second elevator pitch**?
    a. Who are you and what is the **name** of your business?
    b. What **problem** does your product or service solve, or what market void does it fill?
    c. What is your product or service, and how does it **solve this problem** or fill this void?
    d. How is the **world better off** with your product or service than without it?
    e. What amount of **funding** are you looking for and what type of investor are you seeking?

6. Go online and **research three names** for each of the following, and make sure that they are located within 50 to 100 kilometres of your business location.

- ❑ Angel networks
- ❑ Chartered accountants (CAs) you know
- ❑ Lawyers you know
- ❑ Insurance agents you know
- ❑ Financial advisers you know
- ❑ Pitching forums you can attend or enter
- ❑ Business plan competitions you can attend or enter
- ❑ Business incubators you can visit

In this chapter we discussed how finding people who can introduce you to investors is a more productive goal than trying to meet investors directly. In the next chapter, we'll discuss how self-screening your business concept to make sure that it will meet the needs and preferences of investors will improve your chances of attracting investment capital.

CHAPTER 3

DO YOU HAVE A FUNDABLE BUSINESS CONCEPT?

"I think you've got something that may work, and it's going to be four or five years down the road. It looks cute, wild, and woolly ... But the valuation ... you can't even talk about that. It's so ridiculous."
—Dragon to Pitchers

INVESTOR-COURTING STAGE #2: Screening

Self-screen your business concept. Do your research to see the kinds of investments that interest your potential funder. Make sure that your business concept meets investment criteria. Revise and refine your business concept when necessary to make it more attractive to specific investors and customers.

Before there was Juicy Couture (a popular clothing line for women) there was Liz Claiborne. Back in 1976, few women were interested in wearing the pinstripe suits that their male colleagues were used to wearing to work. Women needed to look professional, but didn't want to have to spend hours getting ready. Liz Claiborne knew that a line of business wear for women would level the business playing field in both time-to-dress convenience and professional appeal. But starting a clothing company is a huge undertaking, and next to impossible without funding from some source—even if that source is yourself. So Liz Claiborne put up $50,000 of her own capital, and used that to attract another $200,000 from friends.[1] Her efforts made her the market leader in the United States, and eventually landed her company on the *Fortune* 500 list.

Sadly, Liz Claiborne died in 2007. But in an interesting twist, the company she co-founded—Liz Claiborne Inc.—sold the Liz Claiborne *brand* to JC Penney in 2011. Now

Liz Claiborne Inc. actually sells Juicy Couture. To clear the brand confusion, Liz Claiborne Inc. changed its name to Fifth & Pacific Companies Inc. in May 2012.

Liz Claiborne created a product line that customers connected with on a deep level. Early investors also connected with the line, and they helped Claiborne's business get off the ground. Sometimes investors will make a deal just to be involved in a business that feeds one of their personal passions. That's what happened when MacKenzie & Marr Guitars was pitched in the Dragons' Den using a "blind taste test" style pitch of their $900 guitar against an expensive $5,000 alternative. When one of the Dragons was asked to put on a blindfold and play the competing guitars, he not only sounded pretty good on the MacKenzie & Marr guitar, but he also decided to make an investment.

MACKENZIE & MARR GUITARS

Pitchers: John Marr and Jonathan MacKenzie, Season 4, Episode 13

"Rather than tell you about it, we'd like to show you about it . . . And we understand one of you is a relatively gifted guitar player. And in order to play it fair, we'd like you to apply this blindfold . . . Now you've played two guitars—one of them retails for $5,000, and one of them retails for $900. [You chose our $900 guitar]."
  —Pitcher to Dragons

PRODUCT DESCRIPTION:

Factory-direct acoustic guitars.

DRAGONS' DEN BY THE NUMBERS

- **The Ask:** $35,000 for 35% of the business
- **Company Valuation:** $100,000
- **The Deal:** $15,000 for 5% equity, plus an additional $20,000 for a 7% royalty that decreases to 5% when the three Dragons get their capital back
- **$900:** The price of a MacKenzie & Marr guitar
- **1:** The number of production prototypes that the pitchers brought to the show
- **$0:** Total sales at the time they appeared on the show

Pitchers John Marr and Jonathan MacKenzie demonstrating their $900 guitar that one Dragon chose over a $5,000 version in a blind test.

THE WARM-UP: SCREENING DEFINED

Screening is an analytical process that involves profiling a business concept to make sure that it meets certain minimum criteria that investors need and want. By revising and refining your business concept until it meets these criteria, you'll be much better prepared when you finally get in front of an investor or investor group to make your presentation. The purpose of **self-screening** your business concept in advance is to revise and refine your business idea to make sure that it qualifies as an investment that is attractive to an investor. Screening is a two-stage process:

- **Pre-screening:** An initial evaluation by the investor to see if your proposal matches his or her criteria in terms of the *type of business model*, the *business sector*, or the *stage of your business.*
- **Screening:** An in-depth evaluation to see if your business is *investable*.

Pre-screening: Initial Evaluation

If investors don't understand the industry, geographic region, or target market that you are operating in, then it will be difficult for them to assist you beyond just writing a cheque to fund your business. As a result, many investors set up initial screens, called pre-screens, to weed out business ideas that are not compatible with their own personal investing criteria. In many cases, active investors will even join networks of investors, such as angel networks or investor groups, that do that initial screening for them. Or they may put their money with venture capital firms who do the actual investing for them.

Pre-screening is a smart decision for investors because it keeps them from having to become experts in multiple business types, and leaves them free to focus on becoming more efficient at the ones that they can add value to. Keep this in mind when you find yourself rejected by investors who simply may not have been compatible with you in the first place.

Pre-screening Factors

There are many factors that investors use to pre-screen business ideas, but the list is certainly not exhaustive. Even if your business does not meet their pre-set pre-screening factors, there is always room for a deal if investors find themselves with no other deal flow. The following are factors that investors use to pre-screen investment deals:

- **Industry Sector:** In what industry will your business operate? Many investors avoid industries or sectors that they don't have a history in.
- **Geographic Location:** In what region of the country will your business reside? Many investors don't invest in businesses that they can't visit in person.
- **Funding History:** What funding have you received to date, and what was your valuation at the time? Many investors don't want to invest in businesses that already have other investors involved. Others won't invest in your business if another investor hasn't already endorsed your business concept with a previous investment.
- **Growth Stage:** What is the current status of your business? Many investors only fund a business if it is in a particular stage of growth, such as seed, start-up, early stage, or late stage (see Chapter 1).
- **Source of Referral:** Who introduced you to the investor? Many investors won't even read your executive summary if you weren't introduced by a trusted source.

Pre-screening Methods

As noted, pre-screening is an investor's initial evaluation of your business to determine if it is the type of business or industry that he or she understands or is interested in. Through an online application, over-the-phone Q&A, or in-person verbal presentation, the investor compares your business profile to his or her pre-set business profile (or that of an investor group). Be prepared for an initial evaluation that includes a standardized set of questions using one of the following:

- **Executive Summary:** You submit an executive summary to an investor or an angel network, and they invite you in for a screening meeting if your business fits the pre-screening profile.
- **Elevator Pitch:** You present your business pitch to an investor or investor committee, and, if they like it, they invite you to give a 10- to 15-minute PowerPoint presentation in person.
- **Online Application:** You complete an investor application online through an angel network's website, and then you may be invited to a live pre-screening meeting.

Screening: In-Depth Evaluation

Once investors decide that your business concept is in the right ballpark in terms of its sector and geographic focus, the next phase is to determine if you actually have an investable business concept. Screening, as opposed to pre-screening, is a more formal process that is used to determine if your business will be able to meet the return on investment expectations of the investor. Investing can be a subjective process, but the types of factors that investors look for at this stage of the screening process may include the following:

1. **A Problem:** A burning problem that your product or service solves, or a market void that it fills.
2. **A Solution:** A working prototype of your product, or a sample of your service.
3. **Value Proposition:** Clear proof that the world is better off with your business than without it.
4. **Revenue Model:** A profitable revenue model.
5. **Disruptable Market:** A market sizable enough to provide the investor with a 25% to 50% annualized return and an exit within five to seven years.

6. **Barriers to Entry:** Market entry barriers that can fend off copycat competitors.
7. **Team:** A credible team in place that can implement your business plan successfully.
8. **Scalability:** Ability to handle a sudden increase in customer volume without being constrained by staff or financial-resource limitations.
9. **Business Model:** A sustainable money-making system, not just a short-term product or service fad.
10. **The Deal:** A deal that's worth the investor's time in terms of ROI potential and a reasonable exit strategy within three to ten years at most.

For a more in-depth guide to screening your business concept, consult *The Dragons' Den Guide To Assessing Your Business Concept*.

DRAGON LORE

Self-screen your business concept before you meet investors. Make sure that the investors you spend time courting will be compatible with your business and will see it as an investable business concept.

Products and services don't always have to fit the needs of consumers. You can also target other businesses that have the same need that you do—the need to upsell their products. When the SuperSales Tag was pitched on *Dragons' Den*, the pitchers were wearing their own product—a mini multimedia player that salespeople attach to their shirts.

SUPERSALES TAG

Pitchers: Milad Modir and Jamil Haidari, Season 5, Episode 20

BUSINESS MODEL

The pitchers sell the SuperSales Tag, a wearable multimedia player, to other businesses.

PROBLEM

Salespeople need a marketing tool to upsell products while they are pitching to their prospective customers.

SOLUTION

A miniature multimedia player that can attach to clothing or fixtures and display advertising for almost eight hours on a single charge.

GO-TO-MARKET

Trade-show participants and retail store chains will buy it for their sales reps to wear.

TEAM

Milad Modir and Jamil Haidari were sales consultants at a telecommunications company.

FINANCIALS

The Ask: $100,000 for 20% equity in the company
Company Valuation: $500,000
Revenue: $330,000 in sales to date
The Deal: $100,000 for 35% equity

The SuperSales Tag, a wearable multimedia player, being pitched on *Dragons' Den*.

SELF-STUDY WORKSHOP: Self-Screening

Self-screening involves evaluating your business as if you were an investor looking at it from the outside in. Review your business concept to make sure that it meets the criteria that the particular investors look for. Be prepared for multiple questions and answers during the process.

PRE-SCREENING

1. What is the **industry sector** you are building a business in?
2. What is the **geographic region** that your business operates in?
3. What is your **funding history** and who provided the capital? (Be sure to identify the rounds of funding you've received—seed, angel, etc.)
4. In what **stage** is your business?
   - ❑ Seed
   - ❑ Start-up
   - ❑ Early Stage
   - ❑ Expansion Stage
   - ❑ Late Stage

SCREENING

1. What **problem** does your product or service solve that has not been solved by other offerings on the market?
2. Do you have a working **prototype** and proof that your concept works? Describe your progress.
3. How is the world better off with your product or service than without it? What is your **value proposition**?
4. How do you charge for your product or service? What is your **revenue model**?
5. What is the **size of your market**?
6. What **barriers to entry** are there to entering your market?
7. Who is on your **team**, and why are they critical to the success of your business?

8. Can your business handle a sudden increase in customer volume without being constrained by staff or financial-resource limitations? Is your business **scalable**?

9. Do you have a long-term revenue-earning business, or just a short-term product or service fad? What is your **business model**?

10. Is the deal worth the investor's time in terms of ROI, potential ROI, and estimated value on exit? How will the investor exit the business (i.e., get their money back) within three to ten years? **Who would potentially buy or merge with the business** within the next three to ten years?

Now that you understand how investors weed out incompatible business ideas and unfundable business concepts, it's time to discuss how investors value your business and put together a tentative deal and term sheet to invest in your business. In the next chapter, we'll discuss valuation methods, term sheets, types of capital, and factors that affect the value that investors put on your business.

CHAPTER 4

HOW MUCH CAPITAL WILL YOU NEED?

"These two represent the future of where consumerism is headed."
—Dragon to Dragons

> **INVESTOR-COURTING STAGE #3: Valuation and Funding**
>
> Figure out what your company is worth. Ask for only the capital that you need. Don't look a gift horse in the mouth by getting too greedy.

If you need outside investors and you have a strong belief in your business, you can do a lot with a $6,000 loan from a brother.[1] Back in 1910, Elizabeth Arden put her name on the line, and brought to life her famous mantra: "To be beautiful is the birthright of every woman." She marketed a service concept that she invented, called a "makeover,"[2] and using a loan from her brother, she took a risk in opening her first salon in the heart of the busiest place she could find—New York City. What started out as a salon with a red door, turned into the Red Door Spa and a worldwide cosmetics empire.

The woman who became a cosmetics legend wasn't born Elizabeth Arden. Her name was Florence Nightingale Graham—her birth name—which she stopped using when she adopted her business name, Elizabeth Arden. And she wasn't from New York City, where her first location still stands today on Fifth Avenue, but a small Canadian town, proving that Canadians who get out of their comfort zone are a true source of entrepreneurial spirit.

Elizabeth Arden was a passionate entrepreneur. So is Christine Poirier, who came up with a solution to breastfeeding in public after experiencing the problem firsthand. At first glance, her idea looked like just another blouse with a strategically placed gap—until she was able to convince two Dragons that she had sales and a complete line of products that were worth a second look.

MOMZELLE

Pitcher: Christine Poirier, Season 4, Episode 18

"I designed those tops after the birth of my daughter in 2006 to feel good about breast-feeding in public settings. It's a line of breastfeeding clothing, and they all have [a very discreet breastfeeding] opening."
—Pitcher to Dragons

PRODUCT DESCRIPTION

Maternity wear for easy and discreet breastfeeding.

DRAGONS' DEN BY THE NUMBERS

- **The Ask:** $60,000 for 20% of the business
- **Company Valuation:** $300,000
- **The Deal:** $60,000 for 30% of the business
- **$125,000:** Sales in the first year of business
- **$45:** The retail price for the tops
- **40:** The number of stores that carry the Momzelle line

Pitcher Christine Poirier with her Momzelle product.

THE WARM-UP: VALUATION AND FUNDING DEFINED

Valuation and funding is a multi-stage process that investors follow to put a value on your business, negotiate a term sheet, and provide funding. The valuation stage actually begins when you meet the investor, and is undertaken over time until it is finalized *after* due diligence. The purpose of the valuation and funding process is to provide capital, guidance, and experience to the entrepreneur, in exchange for a return on investment (for example, 25% to 50% annualized return, and exit within three to ten years) for the investor. The process of funding involves the following:

- **Valuation:** Methods for valuing your business, based on an estimate of its earnings potential, a multiplier, and the investor's required rate of return.
- **Funding Types:** Categories of investor funding, based on what the capital is used for.
- **Term Sheets:** A short summary of the valuation of your business, the amount of money to be invested, and the exit or liquidity-event preferences of the investor.

Valuation

In order to determine how much capital they should invest in your business, investors will try to calculate an estimate of what your business is worth. This estimate is called a **valuation**.

This is not a detailed business guidebook on how to value a business. If your intent is to exchange equity for a significant amount of capital, be sure to speak with outside advisers, accountants, and/or lawyers first in order to determine *your* valuation of your business. You should be aware that your figure may be completely different from the valuation made by an investor. For now, it is important to understand the logic behind valuation calculations so that you will understand what is going on during the process. Know that investors won't invest in your business if they can't achieve an attractive rate of return over a given time period. The risk of investing in a business is much too high for an investor to part with his or her cash without an expected annual rate of return, which could be 25% or higher per year.

Earnings-Based Models for Valuing Your Business

There are two types of valuations that you need to understand. A **pre-money valuation** is the value of your business before the investor's capital is injected into it. Once the investor invests capital, you add the investor's capital to your pre-money valuation to get a **post-money valuation**. This is the figure you typically see on *Dragons' Den*. The capital they invest, divided by the post-money valuation, determines the share of the business the pitcher is giving up for the capital. The following are two methods of calculating the pre-money valuation of a business, assuming your business has no significant balance-sheet assets:

- **Earnings Multiple Method:** One of the most common ways that an investor will put a value on your business is an earnings-based model, called a *multiple*. In simple terms, this means that the investor will look at your average annual pre-tax profit, and multiply that figure by a number (for example, three, four, or five times earnings). The number or multiple that is applied is usually a rate that is standard among sales of similar businesses. The investor will then multiply the percentage of equity that he or she is seeking in your business (say, 40%) by the valuation, to come up with the amount that he or she must invest to receive that percentage of your business. Through research, you can determine what multiple is used in your industry.
- **Required Return Method:** Another earnings-based method is called the required return method. You take the average annual profit of your business, and divide it by the return that a typical investor requires (say, 25%). The investor will then add his or her capital to that figure and multiply the result by the percentage of equity he or she is seeking in your business. The result is the amount that the investor must invest to receive that percentage of your business.

In order to calculate a valuation of your business using these two methods, investors must agree on an earnings estimate to use in the calculations—a process referred to as **normalizing earnings**. For example, if you tell an investor that your business earned $300,000 last year, and that you didn't take a salary, the investor will adjust your earnings figure down by a fair salary (say, $80,000 to $120,000). The new earnings figure is then used in the valuation calculation.

Although this is an oversimplification of the valuation process, it does illustrate one key point: the higher the valuation of your business, the more money you should receive from an investor. So, what if you don't have any profit? You and the investor can agree to a profit forecast, or you can use a multiple of revenue as a valuation model instead.

Valuation Terminology

Whether or not you choose to become well versed in valuation, an understanding of the terminology is important during your fundraising efforts.

- **Pre-money Valuation:** The value of your business before the investor's capital is injected into it.
- **Post-money Valuation:** The value of your business after the investor's capital is injected into it.
- **Equity You're Giving Up:** The percentage of your company that you are giving to the investor, which is equal to the investor's capital divided by the post-money valuation.
- **Payback Period:** The amount of time it takes for investors to earn their money back.
- **Deal:** The amount of funding that you receive for your business in exchange for equity or convertible debt. Investors often use convertible debt—debt that can be converted into equity ownership at a later date—to hedge their position in your business. For example, if the business starts to perform well, then the investor has the option of converting the debt that you owe into a share of the business.
- **EBITDA:** Earnings before interest, tax, depreciation, and amortization.
- **Net Income:** The after-tax earnings of a business.
- **Earnings Multiple Valuation Method:** Pre-tax profit of your business times x, where x is the multiple.
- **Revenue Multiple Valuation Method:** Revenue times y, where y is the multiple; the multiple used in the revenue valuation method will be less than the multiple used in the earnings method.
- **Return on Investment (ROI):** The return the investor requires in order to make the investment deal worthwhile, such as an annualized 25% return.
- **Dilution:** The amount that your equity stake in the business is reduced when an investor takes part ownership of the company.

Valuation Examples

Here are some hypothetical numbers that we can use in these example calculations:

- pre-tax profit after founder's fair-market-value salary = $300,000/year
- angel investor's required rate of return = 25%
- typical earnings multiple for this industry = 3

VALUATION EXAMPLE 1: Earnings Multiple Method

Pre-money Valuation

= Pre-tax Profit × Earnings Multiple

= $300,000 × 3

= $900,000

Note: This valuation method completely ignores any liens, debts, or judgments against your business, industry growth rates, and assets (such as cash) on your balance sheet.

VALUATION EXAMPLE 2: Required Return Method

Pre-money Valuation

= Pre-tax Profit ÷ Required Rate of Return

= $300,000 ÷ 0.25

= $1,200,000

Note: This valuation method also ignores any liens, debts, or judgments against your business, industry growth rates, and assets (such as cash) on your balance sheet.

You should calculate your valuation using both formulas above so that you have a range of values for your business that you can compare against what the investor thinks your business is worth. At the same time, always make sure that you and the investor are using the same assumptions in your calculations. For example, the investor's definition of profit may be after your salary is added, while yours may have excluded your salary.

Factors that Affect Valuations

When investors put a value on your business, they try to normalize your earnings. That means they make adjustments to the profit figures you have provided to them in order to make them comparable to other businesses. For example, if you tell them that your profits were $300,000 last year, they'll ask you if you took a salary. If you didn't take a salary, they'll subtract one from the $300,000 to get a more accurate picture of what profit the company would earn when paying a manager. After you take a hypothetical $100,000 salary, your earnings are reduced to $200,000. The following are factors that affect valuations in general:

- **Earnings Adjustments:** If your pre-tax profit (i.e., earnings) reflects expenses that will no longer exist if the investor comes on board, then the earnings figure will go up, as will the valuation. Earnings can be adjusted for a salary for the principal of the company or for an office-rental fee if the owner/entrepreneur has been operating the business out of his or her home.

- **Sector Norms:** A rising tide lifts all boats, so sometimes regardless of what your particular business is expected to generate in terms of revenue or earnings, industry norms will override those expectations. If businesses in your industry normally sell for a certain multiple of earnings that is higher or lower than your estimated valuation, then you will have to explain why your valuation should be different. Be sure to research the standard valuation multiple for businesses that sell in your industry. Speak to your business adviser, a business appraiser or broker, and/or your chartered accountant for their assessment of the multiple to use in your industry.

- **Growth Potential:** If you are in a rapidly growing market, then you can expect the valuation of your business to be a higher multiple of earnings than a slow-growth-industry business would have. That's because the multiple has to keep pace with future expectations of profit and revenue, not just with where the business is now.

- **Asset Adjustments:** If your business has cash or other assets sitting on the balance sheet (RIM recently had around $1.8 billion in cash, yet the company's stock value is in the tank as of this writing), there needs to be an adjustment to the earnings valuation method figure to account for those assets. For example, if your business is worth $1 million based on earnings alone, but you also have $500,000 in cash and no debt, then you might be justified in assuming that your business is worth more than $1 million.

Funding Types

When an investor is interested in your business, they are going to ask what their funds will be used for. As discussed in Chapter 1, you should lay out specific milestones that you are trying to reach with the investment capital. You'll do this in detail in the business plan section of this book. For now, understand that there are two general categories of funding: working capital and growth capital.

Working Capital

Even if you just want to keep your doors open, without necessarily growing, you need **working capital**. Working capital is the money required to pay your expenses less the revenue you have coming in. Your business can't do without working capital, so it should be included as a component of your overall funding request if the cash flow from your business doesn't currently cover your needs. Working capital includes money needed for selling your product or service, and for general and administrative expenses.

There is one caveat when it comes to working capital requests: a funding request made solely to pay your employees' and your salaries will position your business as a lifestyle business that is not a fundable growth business. Ideally, your business plan should use internally generated cash flow to pay for your working-capital needs in the short term, or you won't be in business long.

Growth Capital

Most investors invest based on the **growth capital** needs of a business, not just its working capital needs. Growth capital is meant to fund your next product development project, go-to-market efforts, or some other major initiative. In some cases, it may even pay for buildings, if buying a building is a part of your business model. The underlying purpose of growth capital is to fund projects that will allow your business to meet revenue projections. In the funding-request section of your business plan, be sure to provide a complete list of how and when you plan to spend the capital.

Term Sheet

If all goes well, and if you're dealing with an experienced investor who is ready to invest in your business, the investor will give you a **term sheet**. A term sheet is a document that investors provide you with before due diligence begins, which shows their valuation of your business, the amount of money they are willing to invest, and their exit or liquidity preference (usually after the investors are paid back). It is not a contract, but is the basis for the contract that eventually becomes the deal between you and your investors. This is legal territory, so consult your lawyer prior to signing anything. The following are some of the common terms that the term sheet may contain:

- **Investment Type:** Common shares or convertible debt, for example.
- **Valuation:** An estimation of how much the business is worth, including pre-money and post-money valuations.
- **Amount Invested:** The dollar amount to be invested in your business.
- **Legal Entity:** The legal entity that your current business is (sole proprietorship, partnership, corporation, etc.), or will be upon funding of your business.
- **Investor Names:** Who is investing in your business?
- **Capitalization Table:** How your business is currently funded, and how it will be capitalized after it is funded.
- **Closing Date:** When the deal will close and you will receive your funds.
- **Use of Funds:** The specifics of how you will use the funds invested.
- **Conversion Terms:** Conditions that will trigger the conversion of a loan into equity.
- **Protective Provisions:** Provisions made to protect current investors from new investors.
- **Liquidation Preference:** The priority given to the new investor (over current founders or previous investors) in terms of capital returned and unpaid dividends received in the event of a liquidity event or winding up of the business in the future.
- **Board Representation:** If the investor requires a seat on your board of directors as a condition of investing.
- **Due Diligence Documents:** Guidance as to what documents you will be required to produce during the due diligence process.

DRAGON LORE

Look for an investor, or a combination of investors, who can provide capital, strategic know-how, and industry contacts.

When you're trying to come up with a valuation of your company, you have to make adjustments for your personal salary. The new, lower number comes into play when a valuation is calculated using the earnings multiple method you learned about earlier in this chapter. When pitcher Ryan Foley of NuvoCare Health Sciences showed up on *Dragons' Den*, he found his valuation quickly decreased from $1 million down to $500,000 using some simple calculations and adjustments to earnings by a swift-thinking Dragon.

NUVOCARE HEALTH SCIENCES

Pitcher: Ryan Foley, Season 5, Episode 8

BUSINESS MODEL

Through retail outlets, the company sells a line of all-natural supplements to make people feel and look younger.

PROBLEM

The body ages because of DNA degradation and free-radical accumulation.

SOLUTION

A full line of sleep aids, wrinkle treatments, and weight loss pills.

GO-TO-MARKET

- Available through The Shopping Channel
- Available at 175 GNC stores nationwide
- Contract with the potential to be in 2,700 new stores

TEAM

Founder Ryan Foley from Toronto, Ontario, spent 10 years working for the three largest nutraceutical companies in North America.

FINANCIALS

The Ask: $250,000 for 25% equity in the company
Current-Year Earnings Projection: $125,000 (adjusted down for the owner's salary)
Valuation: $500,000 (four times the company's adjusted earnings)
The Deal: $250,000 for 50% equity in the company

Ryan Foley pitching his line of all-natural supplements to the Dragons.

SELF-STUDY WORKSHOP: Valuation Calculation

Calculate an estimated value for your business. If you are not comfortable with this section, seek advice from an adviser, accountant, or colleague who knows how to do this.

VALUATION

1. What **assumptions** are you comfortable with for each of the following aspects of your business?
   - Pre-tax profit ($/year)
   - Angel investor's required return (%)
   - Business net worth
   - Industry standard valuation multiple

2. What **adjustments** could you make to your pre-tax profit projection if an investor came on board? For example, what salary would need to be paid to someone else to do your job, if you were no longer working in the business?

3. What is a reasonable **valuation** of your business?

- Method 1: Calculate a valuation of your business using the **earnings multiple method** (see Valuation Example 1: Earnings Multiple Method, outlined earlier in this chapter).
- Method 2: Calculate a valuation of your business using the **required return method** (see Valuation Example 2: Required Return Method, outlined earlier in this chapter).
- Method 3: Determine a reasonable valuation of your business by speaking with an **outside adviser** such as an accountant, lawyer, or business adviser.

4. Based on the three valuation methods above, what is the **valuation range** for your business? Take the lowest valuation and the highest valuation that you determined in step 3.

5. What type of **investment capital** are you seeking?
   - ❑ Working capital
   - ❑ Growth capital

6. What will you **use** the capital for?

In this chapter, we discussed methods for valuing your business so that you can come up with a reasonable estimate of how much equity you could give up in exchange for the investor funding you need. Now it's time to discuss how deals fall apart. Due diligence is a process where investors go from weeding through your pitch to weeding through your facts. In the next chapter, we'll discuss how to self-audit your business to make sure that your financial, legal, and operational documents are prepared for an interested investor, so that you end up receiving a cheque.

CHAPTER 5

ARE YOUR ASSUMPTIONS ACCURATE?

"I was going to put $400,000 [up], make sure that *that* $400,000 was spent wisely in terms of the gathering facility, a little bit of travel to do. You've got to tie up contracts. That was the idea. But you stepped up your game. [And] we stepped apart. So the reality is, I'm out."

—Dragon to Pitcher

INVESTOR-COURTING STAGE #4: Due Diligence

Be able to back up your numbers and promises with real facts. Don't create false expectations, because investors can and will verify what you say.

Some entrepreneurs are always on the leading edge, and sometimes they may even be slightly ahead of their time. When Dean Kamen invented the Segway PT, he knew he had revolutionized travel—he just had to convince consumers. Or did he? His idea was so revolutionary that big-league venture capital investors, including Kleiner Perkins Caufield & Byers, collectively backed his invention with over $100 million in funding. But the problem with the early Segway PT model was that no one had ever seen one before, so it took longer than expected to catch on.

Today, Segway Inc. has new owners and has found many applications for its product. The Segway PT is currently being used as a means for tourists to get around in popular tourist destinations around the world, as a patrol unit for cops in places like Vancouver, and as a golf cart for golfers in places like Florida. We are slowly starting to see them in more places, and, though Dean Kamen's prediction that the Segway PT would displace the car may never come true, it is certainly catching on in niche markets. So, did the Segway PT ultimately lead to a return on investment? Well, that depends on whether you are the founder, the investor, or the current owners. And since the company is currently a private one, we'll never know.

As Segway's history shows, business can be a high-stakes game of musical chairs, with some investors feeling like they missed out on a good deal, and others wishing they hadn't invested in the first place. Even if you are fully prepared with an investable business concept, deals fall apart for any number of reasons, sometimes inexplicably. Some entrepreneurs visit the Dragons' Den with all of their i's dotted and t's crossed, and still don't get a deal. Dan Mez, founder of Fitness on the Go, had $850,000 in sales, four established franchises in British Columbia alone, and a "You had me at hello" comment from one of the Dragons for his model-like looks, even before he started his pitch. But all that still wasn't good enough to get a deal.

FITNESS ON THE GO

Pitcher: Dan Mez, Season 4, Episode 8

"My name is Dan Mez. I'm from Vancouver, B.C. The fact is, a lot of people sign up for a gym membership and they never go. But if I came to their house, I knew that they were doing it. Having a personal trainer come to your house to make sure that you're on your schedule works."
—Pitcher to Dragons

PRODUCT DESCRIPTION

Personal trainers who bring their service to their customers.

DRAGONS' DEN BY THE NUMBERS

- **The Ask:** $250,000 for 20% of the business
- **Company Valuation:** $1.25 million

- **The Deal:** $0
- **4:** The number of Fitness on the Go franchises that currently exist in B.C.
- **$850,000:** Sales in Year 3
- **5:** The multiple of earnings that one of the Dragons used to value the business. Ultimately, all of the Dragons felt that the pitcher's valuation was far too high, and the pitcher was unwilling to give up enough equity to meet the Dragons' requirements.

Dan Mez of Fitness on the Go pitching his mobile fitness franchise concept to the Dragons.

THE WARM-UP: DUE DILIGENCE DEFINED

Due diligence is a post-screening process that investors undertake to verify that the investor pitch and business plan you have presented to them is financially, operationally, and legally sound. This is the "dot the i's and cross the t's" part of the investor-courting process. By this point, the investor already believes that you have a great business idea—now he or she just wants to make sure that you have your facts straight.

The purpose of due diligence is for investors to confirm or withdraw their tentative decision to invest, based on what they see in the details of your business plan. The due diligence process, which can take from fifteen days to six months or longer, involves vetting the entrepreneur's business and business plan using the following:

- **Financial Due Diligence:** Reviewing your financial statements to make sure that your projections are realistic.
- **Operational Due Diligence:** Reviewing your business operations to make sure that you can handle the sales volume that is projected in the business plan.

- **Legal Due Diligence:** Reviewing your legal history to make sure that there are no legal land mines hidden in your background.
- **Deal Killers:** Unexpected surprises during the financial, operational, and legal due diligence process that you failed to highlight.

The level of due diligence performed by an investor depends on the investor's financial and emotional tolerance for risk. One investor might request reams of information and follow-up answers, while another might write a cheque without even reading your business plan. If you're lucky enough to be considering investment capital from two different investors, the way you are treated during the due diligence stage may determine whom you eventually get into bed with. On the one hand, detail-oriented, hard-nosed investors, who ask you a million questions, can be annoying at first, but may be just the type of investor you want on your side. They may have the analytical skills you need to bring your business to the next financial milestone, or point you in the right direction. On the other hand, cordial investors who ask for little follow-up beyond your business plan may seem lackadaisical. But maybe they are sophisticated enough to know a good deal when they see one, and could be just the type of investor who will leave you alone to build your business.

Either way, embrace the due diligence process much as you would the screening process—as a way to improve your business. Try to see beyond subjective factors, such as the personality of the investor, and look more at objective factors, such as what that investor brings to the table both financially and strategically.

Financial Due Diligence

Surviving the due diligence process involves being prepared for what an investor *may* ask you for, not necessarily what they *will* ask you for. If you have all of your financial ducks in a row in advance, you'll be better prepared and more confident, and you might just get off easy with a short fact-checking process. Keep in mind that not all requests from an investor may be relevant. If an investor asks you for a three-year history of your business and you just started last week, that's not necessarily a deal killer unless you told the investor you opened your doors three years ago. Just prepare for a detailed evaluation as if you were preparing for a CRA audit. Here are some of the financial documents you should be prepared to explain and/or provide to the investor for viewing:

- **Financial Statements:** A minimum of current balance sheet, up to three years of past and projected profit and loss statements, and three years of projected cash-flow statements.
- **Tax Returns:** Your past two years' tax returns. Sometimes these are requested just to check that you are filing your taxes (to verify that you are not a moral hazard).
- **Payroll Records:** If you have been in business for a while, the investor wants to know that you are compliant and up to date with your employee obligations.
- **Books and Records:** Ledgers, bank statements, and debt statements, to make sure that you can live up to your promises, and that your business doesn't have any outstanding liabilities that you have failed to mention.

Operational Due Diligence

Operational due diligence takes place when the investor visits your business, speaks to your customers and team, and engages your business in person. He or she is looking to see if you can implement your business plan as promised. To be ready for this part of the due diligence process, an investor *may* look for the following:

- **Business Plan:** A business plan to show that you have thought out all aspects of your business, including marketing, finance, operations, and a potential exit in the future.
- **Operations Manual:** An operations manual to show the operating processes and process flow chart you use to produce your product, perform your service, or manage inventory. They also look for proof that your products and services perform as promised.
- **Existing Customers:** A customer list that backs up the amount and kind of business you have done in the past. Also be prepared to have your investor call some of your customers to interview them about their satisfaction with the products or services they purchased from you.
- **Employees:** A list of current, past, and prospective employees. Also prepare your team for potential interviews with the investor and his or her legal team.
- **Team Background:** Confirmation of backgrounds, resumés, references, and experience of each of your key team players, advisory board, and board of directors if you have one.

Legal Due Diligence

Investors also need to know if your business has any legal land mines that you haven't disclosed. For example, if you think you have a patent, but that patent doesn't cover other important countries, then you might not have the sustainable competitive advantage that you think you have. If you think you have a patent, and you only have a trademark, even worse. And if you have liens or judgments against your business that you "forgot" to mention, then your business may be worth significantly less, and you might have killed any chance of a deal. Be prepared to provide the following documents upon request:

- **Contracts, Agreements, and Non-disclosure Agreements:** Legal contracts that you have in place with other people, employees, businesses, or investors.
- **Licenses:** Licenses that you need to run your business, to prove that your business is in good standing with all local, provincial, and federal regulatory departments.
- **Lawsuits, Liens, Judgments, Claims, or Regulatory Violations:** Documentation that supports any outstanding unfavourable legal actions or regulatory violations against your business.
- **Intellectual Property Documents:** Proof of patents, trademarks, and copyrights that you have obtained to protect the intellectual property of your business.
- **Corporate Entity Documents:** Proof that your business has been legally incorporated.

Deal Killers

Due diligence is not a witch hunt, but in some cases, it may feel like it is. Investors are getting into bed with you financially, so they need to know the background of the person they are dealing with. If, for some reason, you have failed to mention something that an investor later uncovers on his or her own, be prepared to renegotiate your deal, or be prepared for the investor to walk away. But if and when this scenario happens, especially if it is due to a true oversight on your part, it isn't the end of the road for you. Just use the experience to do better next time by revising and refining your pitch, and pitching to another investor. Typical deal killers include the following:

- **Financial Due Diligence:** Numbers aren't as represented, or your assumptions are wrong.
- **Operational Due Diligence:** Background check of your team and operations reveals something that wasn't disclosed.
- **Legal Due Diligence:** Expiring intellectual property or undisclosed liabilities.

DRAGON LORE

If luck is when opportunity meets preparation, then due diligence is when preparation is put to the test. When you take on an investor, your business becomes an open book. Be prepared to answer any and all financial, operational, and legal questions from the partner you are about to get into bed with.

No one said pitching to investors is a conflict-free process, but if you have a proven track record and sales, you'll find that investors will want to dig deeper into your business and may be prepared to give you what you need. Pitcher Lorelei Hepburn came to the Dragons' Den with sound credentials—she was trained as an environmental technologist—and a track record of bringing products to market. Her innovative green solution to an age-old problem had all the Dragons wanting to participate in the deal.

NEMA-GLOBE GRUB BUSTERS

Pitcher: Lorelei Hepburn, Season 4, Episode 21

BUSINESS MODEL

The company sells an organic lawn-care product to rid gardens of pests.

PROBLEM

With pesticides outlawed in some provinces, how do you keep your garden green and free of pests?

SOLUTION

The Nema-Globe Grub Buster is a ball made of biodegradable potato starch that contains a package filled with millions of microscopic nematodes that feed on grubs and pests such as ants. She calls them worms with attitude!

GO-TO-MARKET

The go-to-market is two-pronged: direct online sales, and deals with retail giants Home Hardware and Canadian Tire.

TEAM

Lorelei Hepburn is an environmental technologist from Oshawa, Ontario. Her area of expertise is soil, and she has worked with universities to develop a line of organic, pesticide-free lawn-care products.

FINANCIALS

The Ask: $250,000 for 15% equity in the company
Company Valuation: $1,667,000
Current Sales: $1.4 million in the first four months of operation
The Deal: $250,000 for 15% equity in the company, plus 11% royalty until the $250,000 is paid back, and 5.5% royalty in perpetuity

Lorelei Hepburn pitching her worms with attitude.

SELF-STUDY WORKSHOP: Due Diligence Self-Audit

Complete a self-audit of your business to make sure that you are prepared for any and all questions from the investor who has tentatively agreed to fund your business.

1. Which of the following **financial documents** do you currently have in place?
   - ❏ Current balance sheet
   - ❏ Profit and loss statements (three years back if applicable/three years forward)
   - ❏ Personal tax returns (last two years)

- ❑ Payroll records (since you started your business)
- ❑ Ledger
- ❑ Bank statement
- ❑ Loan statements
- ❑ Other

For each financial document that you are missing, explain what you are doing to correct the deficiency.

2. Which of the following **operational documents** do you currently have in place?
   - ❑ Business plan
   - ❑ Operations manual
   - ❑ Customer list
   - ❑ Employee list
   - ❑ Team resumés
   - ❑ Team references
   - ❑ Other

   For each operational document that you are missing, explain what you are doing to correct the deficiency.

3. Which **customers** or suppliers could you make available to investors, if they request an introduction?

4. What have you done to prepare your **employees** for potential interviews with investors?

5. Which of the following **legal documents** do you currently have in place?
   - ❑ Contracts and agreements
   - ❑ Licenses
   - ❑ Documentation of previous lawsuits, liens, judgments, claims, or regulatory violations
   - ❑ Intellectual property documents
   - ❑ Corporate entity documents
   - ❑ Other

   For each legal document that you are missing, explain what you are doing to correct the deficiency.

Okay, that wasn't so bad, was it? A due diligence self-audit is not just something you do to prepare yourself for outside investors. It makes good business sense and can give you the financial, operational, and legal infrastructure you need to grow your business—even if you don't get funded by an investor. Investors only perform due diligence on your business because they want to make sure that your business and their investment don't fall apart. So it's a win-win. If you pass this step of the investor-courting process, then you'll sign legal documents and the investor will write a cheque. It's essential that your lawyer is waiting in the wings to help you finalize terms.

This ends Part I: The Investor-Courting Process. You now have a basic understanding of what investors look for, so now it's time to build your pitch. In Part II: The Business Plan Checklist, we'll discuss how to pitch to an investor using four different methods.

PART II

THE BUSINESS PLAN CHECKLIST

Create an elevator pitch, PowerPoint pitch, and executive summary. Then create the table of contents for your business plan.

CHAPTER 6

PITCHING TO INVESTORS

"What I'd like to do is I'd like to circle [your] presentation around making money. It's very important. And I think we've got to move that ship, guide it in for the landing on the cash . . . How am I going to make money?"

—Dragon to Pitcher

PITCHING TO INVESTORS

A pitch is an interactive discussion with an investor. Focus the core of your pitch on your business model and why the world is better off with your business concept than without it. State clearly how the investor is going to make money.

Almost a century ago, in 1916, an innovative entrepreneur named Clarence Saunders was looking for a way to improve the grocery-shopping experience and generate a healthy profit for his business. He launched a grocery store called the Piggly Wiggly in Memphis, Tennessee, based on a new business model called "self-service" shopping.[1] For the first time, shoppers could pick their own groceries off the shelf, instead of having a clerk do it for them. Not exactly a revolutionary idea by today's standards, but, back then, it was a hit out of the ballpark. Self-service shoppers no longer had to compete with other impatient customers for the attention of a harried clerk. They could shop themselves, pay *cash*, and then *carry* the groceries right out the door. Suddenly the grocery business was scalable, and was so successful that Piggly Wiggly still has over 600 stores today. The business model also inspired other retailers for decades to come.

What was unique about his business was not the products that were being sold, which were commodities, but the business model being used, which was a true innovation. The business model was so simple, yet revolutionary, that it soon made its way north to Toronto. Theodore Loblaw and J. Milton Cork launched their own version of the self-service grocery-shopping business model in Toronto in 1919, and called it Loblaws. And 43 years later, Murray Koffler used the self-service concept to revolutionize the drugstore industry, founding Shoppers Drug Mart in 1962. In fact, so many other businesses followed suit that self-service shopping is now the standard way to shop for groceries, pharmaceuticals, hardware, and most other retail categories. Unless, of course, you shop at Amazon.ca, which, in its way, reverts us to the old process.

If Clarence Saunders were pitching to investors today, he would have a straightforward answer to the question that investors always ask: "What is your business model, and why is it unique?" While you might have a unique product or service, remember that investors are far more interested in your business model, and its underlying "wow" factor, than in a product or service that you think is unique. And that's what the founders of Pook Toques, a successful toque brand, had trouble convincing the Dragons of when they visited the Dragons' Den.

POOK TOQUES

Pitchers: Tony Pook and Kevin McCotter, Season 4, Episode 11

"We have, for the last two years, gone coast to coast at major craft shows. We were picked up by [The] Hudson's Bay Company last year. Our goal isn't just to be a toque and winter-apparel company. We want to model ourselves after the Roots store. Ideally, we want to create a Pook brand. What we've seen is a doubling in revenue each year."
—Pitcher to Dragons

PRODUCT DESCRIPTION

Multi-functional sock hats that are made in Canada.

DRAGONS' DEN BY THE NUMBERS

- **The Ask:** $250,000 for 10% of the business
- **Company Valuation:** $2.5 million
- **The Deal:** $0
- **$400,000:** Sales last year
- **$20:** The approximate retail price of the toques
- **$250,000:** The investment capital that the two entrepreneurs turned down from a Dragon seeking 50% equity

Tony Pook and Kevin McCotter pitching their line of Pook Toques.

THE WARM-UP: PITCHING DEFINED

A pitch is a verbal, visual, or written presentation that describes how you plan to employ your marketing, financial, and team resources to capture a definable market with a profitable product or service. In other words, it's a funding request you make to an investor. The purpose of a pitch is to describe your business model in a way that attracts investment capital from an investor. The following are the elements involved in pitching to an investor:

- **Pitching Formats:** Including the elevator pitch, PowerPoint pitch, executive summary, and business plan.
- **Pitching Guidelines:** Simple rules to follow to keep your pitch on track.

- **Customizing Your Pitch:** Pitch formats are not one size fits all. Many active investors request that you follow their specific requirements. Some investor groups may even request that you fill out an application first. Just be flexible and willing to modify your pitching documents if an investor asks you for a particular format.

Pitching Formats

There are many ways to pitch a business. A pitch can be written, verbal, visual, or a combination of the three. The pitching format you use at any particular time depends on what stage of the investor-courting process you are at. If you have just been introduced to an investor or investor group, then a written executive summary may be requested of you, so that the investor can pre-screen your idea before you meet face to face. If you have been asked to present your pitch in person for the first time during the pre-screening phase, then a verbal elevator pitch with no visual aids may be requested. If you have passed the pre-screening phase, then you may be asked to make a formal PowerPoint presentation to an investor or group of investors so that they can see more numbers. And, finally, if your business has successfully navigated the screening process and the valuation stage, then a detailed business plan will be requested, so that that the investor can confirm that you have worked through all of the details of your venture. Each pitching format has its advantages.

PITCHING FORMATS

Elevator Pitch	PowerPoint Slide Deck	Executive Summary	Business Plan
Informal verbal presentation. Pre-screen presentation to investors. **Length:** 10 to 15 minutes, including Q&A.	Formal verbal and visual presentation. Screening session. **Length:** 15 minutes, including Q&A.	Part of an initial request or application to formally present to an investor or investor group. **Length:** two to three pages at most.	Detailed written plan that is heavily scrutinized during the due diligence stage. **Length:** 10 to 40 pages.

Pitching Guidelines

Regardless of the type of pitch you are making, it will be judged both objectively and subjectively during the process. Objectively speaking, most investors are looking for the same thing—a clear path to a return on investment, with the secondary benefit of being able to get involved with entrepreneurs. Subjectively speaking, their opinion of your investment opportunity will depend on their industry background and an understanding of the sector you operate in.

While pitching to investors is not a professional speaking contest, there are some guidelines that you should keep in mind to enhance your presentation. We won't discuss specific components of each type of pitch here (that's coming up in the next four chapters), but here are some high-level guidelines to keep your pitch on track:

- **Sector Fit:** When possible, learn the backgrounds of the investors you are pitching to so that you can appeal to their personal investment preferences.
- **Business Model:** Be able to clearly explain how and when your business will make money.
- **Feasibility:** Be able to clearly explain why your business concept is technically, market, and financially feasible.
- **Confidentiality**: Don't share any confidential information that you don't want going public. Active investors won't agree to maintain confidentiality, beyond professional courtesy, because of the sheer volume of pitches that they see.
- **Password-Protect Your Documents:** If you email your executive summary, PowerPoint pitch, or business plan, password-protect it and follow up with a call to give the receiver the password.
- **Be Brief, Yet Thorough:** Provide enough information to explain each talking point in your pitch. Avoid long-winded explanations that lose an investor's attention.
- **Be Realistic:** Make sure that your pitch is realistic and based on assumptions you can explain. Outlandish claims about the size of your potential market will destroy your credibility quickly. Know the facts about your market and your competition. The investors don't want to do your homework for you.
- **Expect Immediate Feedback:** Expect investors to freely interrupt your pitch as you're presenting it.
- **Don't Memorize:** Investors can and will throw you off track with impromptu questions during your presentation. Instead of memorizing your pitch, make a list of talking points and understand each point backward and forward, so you'll be able to get right back on track if an investor throws you off with an untimely question.
- **Check Your Grammar:** Have a third party screen your written or visual pitch for any typos or errors.

Customization

Pitching formats are not one size fits all. No two investors are alike, and while some will accept just about any format you give them, others may have an application and/or template for you to follow. For example, while *Dragons' Den* does not accept PowerPoint presentations many other investors prefer this format. Active investors see and hear so many different pitches during the year that they need a way of standardizing them so they can find what they are looking for in an instant. In order to meet this need, be prepared to be flexible when it comes to restructuring your pitch.

The good news is that investors ask a predictable set of questions, so if you put in the groundwork with this book, you should have most of the components you'll need to meet any investor's format.

DRAGON LORE

Pitching formats include business plans, executive summaries, PowerPoint presentations, and elevator pitches. There is no one-size-fits-all approach, and different investors may each request that you fill out their application, and/or reformat your pitch to meet their requirements.

Anyone who is able to charge $700 for a water cooler clearly understands the concept of being an entrepreneur. The team members from Aquaovo have both the entrepreneurial mindset to disrupt a staid market and the managerial skills to implement a sound business plan. And that dual mindset led to a deal when they visited the Dragons' Den.

AQUAOVO

Pitchers: Noémie Desrochers and Vincent Purino, Season 6, Episode 20

BUSINESS MODEL

The company charges $700 for stylish porcelain water-purification systems, and it generates repeat revenue from replacement carbon filters that work with the system. Desrochers and Purino are looking to launch a mass-market, BPA-free plastic model priced at $200 per unit. They also plan to license the product for a 7% royalty to companies in Europe and Japan.

PROBLEM

Plastic water coolers are old-fashioned, ugly, and not eco-friendly.

SOLUTION

An eco-designed tap-water filter and dispenser that is an environmentally secure and stylish alternative to bottled water. The activated carbon filter in the porcelain water dispenser removes anything that tastes or smells funky from the water.

GO-TO-MARKET

The company sells through retailers and directly through a website. The pitchers will license to companies in Europe and Japan.

TEAM

Pitcher Noémie and her brother Manuel (who wasn't present during the pitch) co-founded the company. Manuel designed the product and Noémie's husband, Vincent, is the marketing director.

FINANCIALS

The Ask: $400,000 for 22% equity
Company Valuation: $1.82 million
Current-Year Revenue Projections: $700,000
The Deal: $400,000 for 35% of the company, plus a 3% royalty

Husband and wife team Noémie Desrochers and Vincent Purino demonstrate their luxury water system.

SELF-STUDY WORKSHOP: Pitching

Understand the basic guidelines for pitching to investors. Develop a basic understanding of the pitching formats available.

1. Which of the following **pitches** do you currently have in place?
    - ❑ Elevator pitch
    - ❑ Executive summary
    - ❑ PowerPoint pitch
    - ❑ Business plan

2. What **business sector** are you operating in? (Investors work in industry sectors that they understand.)

3. What part of your pitch would you like to keep **confidential**?

4. What proof do you have that your business plan is **realistic**?

5. Who can review your executive summary, PowerPoint pitch, and business plan for **grammar and typos**?

Investors look for business models, not just innovative products and services. They need to know how you plan to make money, so that they can figure out how they are going to get their investment back with a healthy return. The heart of your pitch, regardless of the format you use, should clearly state what your business model is. In the next four chapters, you'll begin building your pitch, starting with the elevator pitch.

CHAPTER 7

ELEVATOR PITCH

"I think you have a very quick fad. I think you can make a lot of money over a very short period of time. I don't think you have a long, sustainable business. I'm out."
—Dragon to Pitchers

> **PITCH FORMAT #1: Elevator Pitch**
>
> Summarize your entire business plan in a few succinct sentences. Clearly describe your business model and why the world is better off with your business than it is without it. Then tell the investor what you are asking for and why.

Carl von Clausewitz, the nineteenth-century Prussian general and author of *On War*, spoke about a concept later termed *the fog of war*. He explained how, in the heat of battle, military decision makers are surrounded by a fog-like chaos that can render their decision-making ability paralyzed and their plans obsolete.[1] A solution he put forth is to know and aim for the centre of gravity of your enemy when you're on the battlefield.

Now, let's be clear that potential investors are not your enemy. But when they interrupt your pitch, and start peppering you with questions, it may start to feel like the fog of war is enveloping you. At this point, keep in mind that the investor's centre of gravity is his or her need to make money—not to buy your product or service. And *your* centre of gravity is your elevator pitch. If you learn and deeply understand the core elements of your elevator pitch, instead of memorizing them, you can always fall back on the seven talking points that comprise the pitch. An elevator pitch may be as short as 60 seconds, or it may be an 8- to 10-minute (or longer) description of your business model, the capital you need in order to execute it, and the projected path to riches for the investor. Those riches come in the form of an "exit" or liquidity event for the investor in the future. When designed correctly, the elevator pitch should be all you really need to grab an investor's attention.

One family that came to the Dragons' Den with all of their weapons intact was the Kotack family from Cosy Soles. After a nearly flawless elevator pitch, complete with a problem statement, a solution, proof of concept, and a sizable and definable market, they were left stunned when all but one of the Dragons said they shouldn't give up any equity in their business. But they stayed focused, were open to suggestions, and somehow secured a creative deal that you don't often see on *Dragons' Den*.

COSY SOLES

Pitcher: Allan, Patricia, Melissa, Jordan, and Amanda Kotack, Season 4, Episode 11

"I have a neuromuscular disease and one of my symptoms is freezing, painfully cold feet. I tried for years to find anything on the market that would help me. Nothing worked. These slippers have honestly changed the quality of my life. We found out there are millions of people just like me who have cold feet. There's actually 20 million people in the U.S. alone [who] have some form of neuropathy. There's a huge health market for this product."

—Pitcher to Dragons

PRODUCT DESCRIPTION

Patented microwave-heated slippers.

DRAGONS' DEN BY THE NUMBERS

- **The Ask:** $150,000 for 35% of the business
- **Company Valuation:** $428,571
- **The Deal:** $30,000, plus a $120,000 operating line of credit for 10% of the company
- **$700,000:** Sales to date

- **$50:** The approximate retail price of the slippers
- **30,000:** The number of pairs of slippers the family has sold to date

The Kotack family from Cosy Soles arriving in the Dragons' Den.

THE WARM-UP: ELEVATOR PITCH DEFINED

An **elevator pitch** is a short (one- to ten-minute) verbal summary of how your business model is going to change the world, and how the investor can profit from it. The main purpose of an elevator pitch is to secure some type of commitment from the investor, even if it's just a follow-up meeting or a referral to another investor. The process of putting together an elevator pitch involves summarizing your business model in a short compelling statement by following the basic guidelines and format outlined below.

- **Presentation Guidelines:** Try to adhere to some straightforward guidelines when you are developing your pitch.
- **Pitch Format:** An elevator pitch is really just a set of talking points that you try to communicate during your time with an investor. If the investor is not interrupting you, then he or she is probably not interested.

Presentation Guidelines: Elevator Pitch

What if Steve Jobs were alive today, and you were given an extraordinary opportunity to pitch your new product or service idea to him in 60 seconds? Your pitch would have to have a "wow" factor that grabbed his attention fast, because of the number of innovations that he saw developed during his lifetime. You'd be pressed for time because of who he was, so you'd want to make sure that you touched on your critical, specific talking points. You'd know that he was not going to write you a cheque on the spot, so you'd have to make it your goal to get another meeting. And you wouldn't want to blow your once-in-a-lifetime opportunity by fumbling through a pitch that you didn't know inside and out, so you'd have to make sure that you were adequately prepared. Here are some general guidelines:

- **Talking Points:** Develop a short list of seven talking points that reflect the pitch format in the next section. Make sure that you can condense each talking point down to one sentence, so that all seven talking points can be communicated in 60 to 90 seconds. Also make sure that you have supporting information for each talking point, in case you are asked to elaborate during a question and answer period.
- **Brand Story:** Connect to the investor by telling the story of how your product or service came about, not just what your product or service is.
- **Metaphors:** Use metaphors when possible to give context to each of your seven talking points.
- **"Wow" Factor:** Make sure that your talking points communicate the "wow" factor of your business model, and not just meaningless information.
- **Proof:** Provide proof that your product or service will work. Use a live demo, satisfied test customers, credible revenue figures, or credible market research when possible.
- **Credibility:** Maintain your credibility by avoiding outlandish claims.
- **Call to Action:** Find a way to call the investor to action, whether it's through a funding request, a request to meet again, or even an introduction to another investor.

Pitch Format: Elevator Pitch

An elevator is a metaphor for the type of environment you could find yourself in while you are pitching your business concept to an investor—an environment with no PowerPoint, no demo, and very little time. Imagine stepping into an elevator with a potential investor. You have to quickly touch on all the highlights of your business model before the doors open again and the investor gets off. In reality, it may feel more like a phone booth, because active investors who see many pitches may give you little or no room for error, and expect to hear what they need to hear in 60 seconds. But the verbal presentation of your business concept could end up lasting eight to ten minutes, or longer if you are lucky. And just like on *Dragons' Den*, you have to assume that any investor you speak with will have no prior knowledge of your business idea. So be sure to know your elevator pitch cold in case you are interrupted during your pitch.

The length of an elevator pitch depends on the investor you are speaking with. If you only have a few minutes with an investor, then you'll want to stick to a 60-second format complete with a description of your business model and a specific funding request. If you are given eight to ten minutes or longer in front of a group of investors, then you can expand each talking point with supporting information, and include a live demo, a PowerPoint, market stats, and a more detailed discussion of your financials. While there is no standard format for an elevator pitch, the following are seven talking points that you should touch on, preferably in this order:

1. **Problem Statement:** State the market problem or market void that you are trying to fill.
2. **Solution (Product or Service):** Explain your product or service and how it works.
3. **Value Proposition:** Describe what makes your product or service unique and valuable to customers.
4. **Market Opportunity:** Define the size of the market opportunity and your go-to-market strategy for capturing that market.
5. **Revenue Model:** State how you plan to make money.
6. **Proof:** Provide proof that your product or service works and will sell.
7. **Call to Action:** State how much funding you are looking for, what you will use it for, and what you will give up in exchange. Or, request a follow-up meeting if the investor is interested, but noncommittal.

DRAGON LORE

Your elevator pitch will go downhill fast if you are unable to clearly explain how your business will make money. Make sure that the elements of your pitch reinforce your business model, and emphasize how the investor will make money by investing in it.

If you can't get investor capital, bank financing may be your only option. The problem with bank financing is that if you fail to meet repayment terms, the bank may call your loan. When you borrow money from an investor, however, they have a stake in the business with you, but existing debt may pre-screen you out of the running. When pitcher Jacqueline Sava made her first appearance on *Dragons' Den*, her $300,000 outstanding loan was seen as a liability by some of the Dragons.

SOAK WASH INC.

Pitcher: Jacqueline Sava, Season 4, Episode 3

BUSINESS MODEL

The company designs, markets, and distributes an eco-friendly line of no-rinse liquid laundry soap.

PROBLEM

Delicates get damaged when you wash them in the washing machine.

SOLUTION

Premium no-rinse liquid laundry soap for hand-washing delicates like bras and underwear.

GO-TO-MARKET

Soak Wash Inc. sells through retailers, including lingerie shops, yarn shops, quilting shops, and apparel shops.

TEAM

Founder Jacqueline Sava has a bachelor of fine arts in industrial design.

FINANCIALS

The Ask: $300,000 for 25% equity in the company
Company Valuation: $1,200,000
Revenue Last Year: $400,000
The Deal: $0

Jacqueline Sava (left) pitching her product, Soak Wash.

SELF-STUDY WORKSHOP: Creating an Elevator Pitch

You have 60 seconds or less to convince an investor that you have a business model concept worth listening to. What are you going to say?

PRE-WORK

1. You can learn a lot about pitching just by **watching *Dragons' Den***. While you're watching the next episode on TV, or online at www.cbc.ca/dragonsden, judge each pitch as it happens. Look to see if the pitcher covers the following **seven talking points,** and whether the pitch ends up getting funded.

   - ❑ Problem statement
   - ❑ Solution
   - ❑ Value proposition
   - ❑ Market opportunity
   - ❑ Revenue model
   - ❑ Proof
   - ❑ Call to action

2. Visit **www.ted.com** and watch five presentations in any category that interests you. These are not investor pitches, but they can help you hone your stage presence. While watching each presentation (of 18 minutes or less), make note of the stage presence and tone of the person making the presentation.

DEVELOP YOUR PITCH USING SEVEN TALKING POINTS

1. **Problem Statement:** What problem are you trying to solve, or what need are you trying to fill?

2. **Solution:** What is your product or service and how does it work?

3. **Value Proposition:** How does your business model uniquely solve the problem?

4. **Market Opportunity:** What is the size of the market that you are trying to capture?

5. **Revenue Model:** How do you expect to make money?

6. **Proof:** What proof do you currently have that your business model will succeed?

7. **Call to Action:** How much funding are you requesting, what will it be used for, and what are you giving up in exchange?

TEST YOUR PITCH

1. Investors may interrupt you during your pitch and ask you questions. In order to prepare yourself, **randomize** your pitch. Ask someone you know to ask you the previous seven questions in a random order. Try to repeat your answers three to ten times per question, or until you can give succinct, one-sentence answers for each question.

2. Does your pitch have no more than **seven talking points**?

   ❑ Yes

   ❑ No

3. Have you used any **metaphors**?

   ❑ Yes

   ❑ No

4. Does your pitch communicate a **"wow" factor**?

   ❑ Yes

   ❑ No

5. Does your pitch demonstrate **proof** that your business model will work?

   ❑ Yes

   ❑ No

6. Have you removed any and all **outlandish claims**?

   ❑ Yes

   ❑ No

7. Does your pitch have a specific **call to action**?

   ❑ Yes

   ❑ No

The purpose of an elevator pitch is to grab an investor's attention so that he or she offers to fund your business or to meet with you again for a more detailed presentation. Once you get that attention, it's time to show the investor more details, facts, and figures. These can be presented in the form of a PowerPoint pitch, which we'll discuss in the next chapter.

CHAPTER 8

EXECUTIVE SUMMARY

"You're in the business, you're running it, and you know your numbers, and that's what I like."
— Dragon to Pitcher

PITCH FORMAT #2: Executive Summary

Summarize your business plan in two pages. Create an executive summary *before* you create your full business plan. Then, after you have completed your full plan, return to your executive summary to revise and refine it.

You can start a business doing just about anything. Just make sure that your business has a sound business model and a unique feature that helps you stand out from the clutter of your competition. That's what two Harvard Business School graduates knew when they entered their school's annual business plan competition. Their idea? To hold mud-filled obstacle course events around the world, each designed by the United Kingdom Special Forces. Participants are covered in mud as they run, swim, and climb through the 15-kilometre-plus obstacle course. They call their company Tough Mudder, and if you haven't heard of it, you soon will. What started out with $8,000 in funding has resulted in a reported $25 million in projected revenue for 2011.[1] This type of business has formed the basis for an entirely new industry—the obstacle course industry.

But you don't need a "wow" factor like Tough Mudder has to secure an offer from an investor. You just need to be able to communicate the financial, market, and technical feasibility of your business model in the form of a two-page executive summary. Or just visit the Dragons' Den, like the inventors of Travel Roller did, with proof that your business already works. When the inventors of Travel Roller visited the Dragons' Den, they had already launched the prototypical garage start-up, having produced 15,000 units of their massage tool in their garage. With proof like this in hand, and pure confidence in their business, they had the strength to turn down a deal from the Dragons of $125,000 for 50% of their company.

TRAVEL ROLLER

Pitchers: Arysta Bogner-Wood and Adam Wood, Season 6, Episode 13

Focus: Create a Business Plan

"[We] hand-built the original Travel Rollers in our garage in 2007. We actually built over 15,000 units as we were working on the true Travel Roller that we are presenting to you. It is a featured item in national retail chains. It has a stiff inner core and it does not break down. We are into Fitness Depot in 36 stores. We are very well established in Calgary . . . and we just got into Sport Chek."
    —Pitcher to Dragons

PRODUCT DESCRIPTION

An all-in-one massage tool.

DRAGONS' DEN BY THE NUMBERS

- **The Ask:** $125,000 for 25% of the business
- **Company Valuation:** $500,000
- **The Deal:** $0
- **30,000:** The number of units sold to date
- **$40–$80:** The price range of the Travel Roller kit
- **$300,000:** Revenue projected for this year

Arysta Bogner-Wood and Adam Wood pitching their Travel Roller.

THE WARM-UP: EXECUTIVE SUMMARY DEFINED

An **executive summary** is a one- to two-page written summary of how your business concept is going to impact the world, and how the investor can profit from it. The main purpose of an executive summary is to secure a formal investor presentation meeting with an investor, not necessarily to get funded. Investors request executive summaries so that they can pre-screen a business idea before they meet you face to face. To make sure that your summary stays focused on what's important, think about the following:

- **Presentation Guidelines:** Try to adhere to some straightforward guidelines when you are developing your pitch.

- **Presentation Format:** The executive summary can be a stand alone, one-to two-page document, with section headlines that you send to investors in advance of your presentation. At the same time, the executive summary forms the first section of your full business plan.

Presentation Guidelines: Executive Summary

To increase the odds that your executive summary will stand out, here are some guidelines:

- **Length:** Make it no more than 5% to 10% of the length of your full business plan. Try to max out at two pages in total, with no appendices.
- **Sequence:** Present information in the order in which you present it in your full business plan.
- **Action:** Include enough information that an investor will be able to make a yes/no decision, pending a face-to-face investor presentation and due diligence of your full-length business plan.
- **Focus:** Only include information that highlights your business plan. If the investor wants more detail, he or she can ask you and/or read your full business plan.
- **Stand-Alone vs. Section 1.0:** The executive summary can be a stand alone, one- to two-page document, complete with section headings. Alternatively, the executive summary can be the first section of your full business plan.

Presentation Format: Executive Summary

There is no standard format for an executive summary, and yours will vary depending on who is requesting it. For example, if you are seeking capital from a family member or friend, then it's likely that any format will do, including the one you'll find in the workshop in this chapter. But if you are pitching to a network of angel investors, a business plan competition, or even a bank, you may need to modify to fit their format.

Start by producing a base plan with the Self-Study Workshop: Creating an Executive Summary, which you'll find later in this chapter, and then reformat it if requested. While the format will vary, you should have four or five paragraphs, which should consist of the following:

- **Opening Paragraph:** The background of your business and why it is so unique.
- **Business Model Paragraph:** The problem or gap in the market you are addressing, your product or service solution, and your revenue model.

- **Market Opportunity Paragraph:** The size of the market opportunity, your competitive landscape, your go-to-market strategy, and any barriers to entry.
- **Team and Strategy Paragraph:** A one-sentence background of each founder and management and advisory team member.
- **Financial Summary Paragraph:** Your financial highlights, funding request, planned use of proceeds, exit options, and any previous rounds of funding.

Keep in mind that none of these tools: the Executive Summary, PowerPoint presentation, or even a business plan are allowed in front of the Dragons. You are there to verbally pitch your idea, and physically demonstrate your product or service. But these are all tools that you will be asked for if you end up spending significant time pursing investors. And the Dragons themselves will probably ask for them if you are lucky enough to enter the due diligence phase, after striking a deal on the show.

DRAGON LORE

Anyone who tells you there is a standard format for an executive summary is misleading you. Executive summary formats vary based on who is reading the document. Create a prototype executive summary using the workshop at the end of this chapter. Then modify your format *if* an investor, investor group, business plan competition, or bank requests a different format.

The most effective executive summaries contain actual proof that your business model works or will work. And there is no better way to prove that a business model works than to show projected profits on your profit and loss statement. When the founders of Massage Addict Inc. visited the Dragons' Den, they had a proven franchise business model, they had high revenue, and they knew what their business was worth. They were so prepared that they initially rejected all offers that the Dragons put on the table, because they didn't receive what they perceived to be the correct valuation of their business. But, at the suggestion of one of the Dragons, after some time in the dark, they came up with a counter-offer that helped them secure their deal.

MASSAGE ADDICT INC.

Pitchers: Lori MacKenzie and Chris Harker, Season 6, Episode 13

BUSINESS MODEL

The pitchers created a membership-based massage therapy franchise.

PROBLEM

Going to a massage therapist once or twice a week can get quite expensive.

SOLUTION

Canada's first membership-based massage therapy clinic, where customers pay a monthly membership fee to receive a lower rate on monthly massages.

GO-TO-MARKET

Located in shopping plazas (a.k.a. strip malls), which tend to have lower rent and more vacancies than traditional shopping malls.

TEAM

Lori MacKenzie created the company after she injured her back a few years ago and grew frustrated by the high prices of ongoing therapy.

FINANCIALS

The Ask: $125,000 for 10% equity in the company
Company Valuation: $1,250,000
Revenue: Their highest grossing franchisees bring $1 million each year
The Deal: $125,000 for 20% equity

Lori MacKenzie and Chris Harker entering the Dragons' Den to pitch their membership-based message therapy franchise.

SELF-STUDY WORKSHOP: Creating an Executive Summary

Create the talking points of your executive summary by answering the questions in this workshop. Then format your paragraphs into a two-page document using the executive summary format in the appendix of this book. Here are some simple guidelines:

- Limit your document to two pages. Do not include a cover page or attachments.
- Answer the questions in this workshop with one or two complete sentences per question.
- Thread your sentences together into paragraphs, and your paragraphs into an executive summary using the executive summary format in the appendix of this book.
- Be prepared to modify your executive summary as needed to meet customized requests from investor groups, banks, or business plan competitions.

OPENING PARAGRAPH

Limit yourself to one sentence for each talking point when possible.

1. **Business Overview:** What is the name of your company, what does your business do, when did you start, and what is the most amazing thing about your business concept?

BUSINESS MODEL PARAGRAPH

Limit yourself to one or two sentences for each talking point when possible.

1. **Problem:** What problem does your product or service solve?
2. **Product or Service:** What is your core product or service, how does it work, and why is it valuable?
3. **Revenue Model:** How do you plan to make money?

MARKET OPPORTUNITY PARAGRAPH

Limit yourself to one or two sentences for each talking point when possible.

1. **Market Opportunity:** What is the size of the market for your product or service?
2. **Competitive Landscape:** Who are your competitors and what is the sustainable advantage you have over them?
3. **Market Segments:** Who are your potential customers?

TEAM AND STRATEGY SUMMARY PARAGRAPH

Limit yourself to one or two sentences for each talking point when possible.

1. **Team and Advisers:** Who is on your team and what domain expertise and deep market experience uniquely qualify them to execute the plan?
2. **Go-to-Market Strategy:** Who are your customers? How do you plan to get customers? What strategic partners can help you go to market faster?
3. **Proof:** What financial, technical, or market milestones have you reached that prove that your concept will work?

FINANCIAL SUMMARY PARAGRAPH

Limit yourself to one or two sentences for each talking point when possible.

1. **Financial Summary:** Insert a graph of your three- to five-year financial highlights, plus provide full statements for the last three years if you have them.

FINANCIAL SUMMARY

	Year 1	Year 2	Year 3	Year 4	Year 5
Revenue					
Cost of Goods					
Gross Margin					
Operating Expenses*					
EBITDA					

*excluding depreciation and amortization

2. **Funding Request:** How much capital do you need? What are you willing to give up? What will you use the funds for?
3. **Exit Strategy:** What options do you (or the potential investor) have for an exit in the future? Who could potentially acquire your business?

After the investor reviews your two-page executive summary, he or she will ideally ask you to make a formal investor presentation. A formal investor presentation can be given in the form of a live face-to-face meeting, complete with a PowerPoint presentation, which we'll discuss in the next chapter.

CHAPTER 9

INVESTOR PRESENTATION

"One of the things you need to do before you talk to investors is do some background research on them . . . You need to know when you are talking to an investing group, it doesn't matter what the noise is, if someone says there's money on the table, you need to pay attention."

    —Dragon to Pitcher

> **PITCH FORMAT #3: The Investor Presentation**
>
> Summarize your business plan using a slide deck of 10 to 15 slides for the investor presentation. An investor presentation is an opportunity to present the highlights of your business plan using an expanded elevator pitch, a slide presentation, a live demo, and a Q&A.

The purpose of a slide presentation is to present the highlights of your business plan, not to replace it. But don't take my word for it. Talk to Robert Gaskin, the man who invented PowerPoint software. Back when he conceived of the idea for PowerPoint, he saw a future without overhead projectors and transparencies. He needed a business plan to commercialize his invention, so he put together one that was 50-plus pages long, and then summarized the highlights in a 12-slide presentation using his own product—PowerPoint software.[1] His company was later acquired by Microsoft, and the rest (which includes a long line of boring speeches driven by people who insist on reading their slides instead of using them to *support* their presentations!) is history.

    Look, it's not going to hurt anyone to create a 10- to 40-page business plan detailing a business concept and strategy, complete with impressive diagrams, charts, and text. It's an important exercise that you will go through later in this book. But if you can't identify the highlights of your business plan in 10 to 15 short slides *before* you start your business plan, then your plan is probably far too complicated for investors to grasp, or even consider. The key to grabbing an investor's attention is to communicate a clear, concise message in a very easy to understand visual presentation. And that's the key benefit of PowerPoint.

These days, slide shows are a required tool when pitching to investor groups or active investors. They allow investors to standardize the pitches they see so they can make rapid screening decisions. But the downside of a slide show is that it detracts from a live demonstration of your product or service. In fact, these slide shows are absolutely forbidden on *Dragons' Den*. The Dragons are a difficult group to impress, so when the inventors of the Skrapr visited the Dragons' Den, they showed up with a stove, a mini glass window, a blowtorch, and no PowerPoint. And they left with $250,000 in funding.

THE SKRAPR

Pitchers: Richard Lambert and Tony Warns, Season 5, Episode 20

"The biggest problem in a glass-top stove is [that] this is what you are using [a regular scraper that scratches the surface]—everybody uses it, it scratches, people try to return the glass top . . . there's no warranties on it. What we've invented is a scraper that does not scratch. They work on painted windows, hardwood floor, tiles, granite . . . without scratching."
—Pitcher to Dragons

PRODUCT DESCRIPTION

A scraper that can remove baked-on food from glass and other hard surfaces without scratching.

DRAGONS' DEN BY THE NUMBERS

- **The Ask:** $250,000 for 5% of the business
- **Company Valuation:** $5 million

- **The Deal:** $250,000 for a 5% royalty until the capital is recouped, plus 5% equity
- **$3,000,000:** Projected sales this year
- **$2:** The cost to manufacture the Skrapr
- **$15:** The approximate retail price of a Skrapr

Richard Lambert and Tony Warns pitching their Skrapr.

THE WARM-UP: INVESTOR PRESENTATION DEFINED

An investor presentation is a 10- to 15-minute verbal and visual presentation of how your business model is going to succeed, and how the investor can profit from it. The main purpose of an investor presentation is to secure funding interest from investors. To guide you through the process, we'll review presentation guidelines and format.

- **Presentation Guidelines**: Modify your presentation to adhere to the guidelines of the investor you are pitching to.
- **Presentation Format**: Prepare your presentation with an elevator pitch (expanded), slide show, live demo, and a Q&A.

Presentation Guidelines: Investor Presentation

Imagine sitting through a PowerPoint presentation, complete with slides, graphics, and a presenter who reads each slide one by one. You, like an investor, would probably lose interest pretty quickly. While a great investment opportunity can certainly overcome a weak presentation, try not to do anything that could detract from your presentation. On *Dragons' Den*, the Dragons don't know anything about the pitchers prior to the presentation. And on the show, the presentation is the only shot that pitchers get at impressing the Dragons—supporting materials aren't allowed. However, when you go to meet a potential investor, you can start by knowing what each type of investor might request.

- **Individual Investors:** They may allow you to give your elevator pitch during your first meeting with them. They may ask you to email your executive summary and/or business plan before you see them next. If they like what they see, they might let you make a formal investor presentation.
- **Friends and Family:** They will probably accept any format you give them, unless they are active investors. In some cases, an elevator pitch may be enough to secure funding because they already trust you.
- **Business Plan Competitions:** They may ask for an executive summary and a separate bio for each of the founders as part of the competition. Those business concepts that are judged to be appropriate for the next round may then be requested to submit a more detailed business plan and a 10- to 15-slide PowerPoint presentation.
- **Investor Groups:** They may request that you email your executive summary first with an application. If your executive summary looks interesting, they may invite you in to present your elevator pitch to a pre-screening committee. If you pass that pre-screen, then you may be invited for a formal investor presentation, complete with an expanded verbal elevator pitch, a slide presentation, and a detailed business plan to leave behind if any investors become interested.

Presentation Format: Investor Presentation

In an ideal world, you wouldn't need an investor presentation. Your product or service would be so compelling that the investor would simply write a cheque after hearing your elevator pitch. That certainly has happened in the investment world, as it has so often in the Dragons' Den. But investors are becoming increasingly sophisticated, and with that comes a more intense screening process.

Elevator Pitch (Expanded): 10 to 15 Minutes

An investor presentation is really an expanded version of an elevator pitch. When we discussed your elevator pitch in Chapter 8, we went over the seven talking points that you need to communicate. During the investor presentation you'll have a little more time, so you'll be able to touch on those seven talking points plus a few more. By now you should know your elevator pitch backwards and forwards, so during this chapter's workshop, you can use its contents to create the slides for your slide show.

Slide Show: Visual Support

You can design your slide show presentation for free using an online program like Google Docs (you can sign up for a free account at docs.google.com) or you can use a commercial program like Microsoft PowerPoint or Apple's Keynote software. The key to an investor presentation slide show, also known as a slide deck, is to keep each slide very simple using these guidelines:

- **Business Plan Highlights:** Highlight one section of your business plan on each slide. Provide the investor with a copy of your business plan prior to or just after the presentation if they want more details.
- **Limit Content:** No more than 10 to 15 slides in total, no more than one or two images/charts per slide, and no more than seven talking points per slide.
- **Visual Aid Only:** Use a slide show as support for your verbal presentation, not as a replacement for it. Know your talking points and be able to deliver them without a slide show if you have to.
- **Readability:** Use readable fonts like Times New Roman or Arial, just like you would in a book. Also choose one background to use throughout the presentation to maintain visual continuity.

Live Demo: Presentation Support

If a picture is worth a thousand words, then a demonstration is worth a thousand pictures. How can you possibly explain the Kelvin.23 multi-purpose tool from Season 4, Episode 12 without showing it to an investor? Or how could you truly explain how Notewagon from Season 6, Episode 6 helps students buy class notes from other students, without a live demo of your website? Once you have finished explaining the pain point that your product or service solves, it's time to describe how your product or service works. But you shouldn't spend the majority of your investor presentation on a live demo—spend two to three minutes at most, and only if the nature of your product or service lends itself to a quick live demonstration. Otherwise, tell a story instead. (For more on describing your product, read *The Dragons' Den Guide to Assessing Your Business Concept*.) You can always schedule a follow-up meeting with investors later if they want more detail. Ensure that you describe the following elements:

- **Trigger Events:** The problem or event that leads to someone requiring your product or service.
- **Step-by-Step Operation:** How your product or service works to solve that specific problem.
- **Environment:** The place where your product or service will be used or experienced by your customer.

Q&A: 10 to 15 Minutes

A question and answer session (Q&A) may take place during or after your presentation. Typically, for formal investor networks, the Q&A will happen during the second half of your presentation. But with individual investors and their advisers, the Q&A might be a rapid-fire exchange that interrupts your pitch on a slide-by-slide basis. Be prepared for either. The types of questions you'll receive are the topics of the slides themselves, so if you have prepared your slide presentation carefully, you should have no problem giving answers.

> **DRAGON LORE**
>
> Learn the backgrounds of the investors you are pitching to, so that you understand the strategic value they could bring to a deal, above and beyond the financial capital.

The type of business you enter can sometimes hit a nerve with investors. Start a triple-bottom-line business, and some investors will be so touched by your desire to help people and save the planet that they'll write you a cheque. But start a business like a collection agency, and your reception might not be as warm and fuzzy. When Deborah Maloney visited the Dragons' Den looking for funds for her collection agency, she hit a nerve so deep that only one investor, who truly loves money, was willing to stand by her idea and offer her a deal.

THE LAW OFFICES

Pitcher: Deborah Maloney, Season 6, Episode 7

BUSINESS MODEL

A debt-collection agency that buys debt of U.S. companies and citizens for two to five cents on the dollar. Collectors then collect the balances in full on the accounts.

PROBLEM

How to turn five cents into one dollar with one phone call.

SOLUTION

Buy U.S. debt for two to five cents on the dollar, and then collect it from the debtors. Because the company resides in Canada and is collecting in the United States, it can use a name that encourages people to pay up: The Law Offices. If a company called The Law Offices calls you up about a debt, you might be inclined to respond more quickly than if the caller is immediately identified as a debt collector.

GO-TO-MARKET

The pitcher solicits debt from corporations that have not been paid nor sent their debt out to a collection agency. In some cases, Maloney will work on a contingency basis.

TEAM

Deborah Maloney runs what she calls "one of the most successful debt-collection agencies in Canada."

FINANCIALS

The Ask: $500,000 for 33% equity in the company
Company Valuation: $1.52 million
Revenue: Collected $675,000 in debt in an eight-month span
The Deal: $500,000 for 50% equity

Pitcher Deborah Maloney explains her business model to the Dragons.

SELF-STUDY WORKSHOP: Creating an Investor Presentation

Draft the content of your slide presentation using this workshop. Then use a slide show program like Google Docs (free), Microsoft PowerPoint, or Apple Keynote to bring your slides to life. For each slide, try to stick to a headline, a few bullet points if necessary, and a diagram or two if the diagram is absolutely critical. Typically, the first three slides should be your title slide, problem slide, and solution slide. But then you can modify the order of the rest based on the specifics of your business model.

TITLE SLIDE

Slide 1: Title

List your business name, logo, and contact information.

BUSINESS MODEL SLIDES

Slide 1: Problem

What's the customer problem that you are solving with your product or service?

Slide 2: Product or Service

What is your core product or service? What is your value proposition? What tangible results will the customer get for the money? Why is the world better off with your product or service than it is without it?

Slide 3: Revenue Model

How do you plan to make money? What are your revenue streams?

MARKET OPPORTUNITY SLIDES

Slide 1: Market Opportunity

What is the size of the market that you are able to service?

Slide 2: Competitive Landscape

What are the barriers to entry into your industry? Who are your competitors, and what sustainable advantage do you have over them?

Slide 3: Market Segments

Who are your potential customers?

TEAM AND STRATEGY SLIDES

Slide 1: Team and Advisers

Who is on your team, and what domain expertise and deep market experience uniquely qualify them to execute the plan? Do you have any external advisers or board members?

Slide 2: Go-to-Market Strategy

Who are you customers? How do you plan to get customers? What strategic partners can help you go to market faster?

Slide 3: Proof

What financial, technical, or market milestones have you reached that prove that your concept will work?

FINANCIAL SLIDES

Slide 1: Financial Highlights

Give a three- to five-year financial projections summary (as well as full financials for the past three years if possible).

FINANCIAL HIGHLIGHTS

	Year 1	Year 2	Year 3	Year 4	Year 5
Revenue					
Cost of Goods					
Gross Margin					
Operating Expenses*					
EBITDA					

*excluding depreciation and amortization

Slide 2: Funding Request

Funding to date, funding requested, equity offered (common, preferred stock, or convertible debt), and planned use of new funds.

Slide 3: Exit Strategy

Potential acquirers, strategic investors, or liquidity events in the future.

An investor presentation gives you the opportunity to demonstrate your product or service, back up your presentation with facts and figures, and answer questions that investors will ask you. The next stage in the process is to create an actual business plan, which we will discuss in the next chapter.

CHAPTER 10

BUSINESS PLAN BLUEPRINT

"Success is not a God-given right. Everybody's got kids. Everybody's made sacrifices to get up here. I raised my kids. I worked two jobs. You do what you have to do."
— Dragon to Pitcher

> **BUSINESS PLAN BLUEPRINT**
>
> Define your product and business. Identify your market and your competition. Establish a sustainable business model and rapid go-to-market strategy. Develop defensible financial projections. Put a qualified team in place to execute the plan. Then write it up in the form of a well-written planning document so you can share your vision with investors, banks, and other stakeholders.

Trying to create a business plan while learning all of the terminology can be like drinking water from a firehose. You are an expert in your business, and most likely don't have time to learn about valuations, term sheets, and funding requests. But you do need to understand every decision you make, even if you've hired someone else (like a business consultant, business appraiser, or chartered accountant) to help you create the required documents. Just like your financial adviser tells you never to invest in something you don't understand, you should never enter into an investment deal that you don't understand. A bird in the hand can be worth two in the bush, so sometimes the best deal you'll find is right in front of you.

If you do end up in front of an investor who shows an interest in your business, be sure to act fast. Investors can change their minds on a whim, and a deal that appears to be on the table might disappear in a flash—as the owner of Dans un Jardin found out when he was inches away from closing a $500,000 deal with a Dragon. When the pitcher hesitated, the Dragon changed his mind.

DANS UN JARDIN

Pitcher: Martin Gagne, Season 6, Episode 15

"This is the first automatic vending machine for liquid laundry detergent. With this machine, you reuse your bottle. The first bottle will cost you $7.99, and your refill will cost you $6.99. You save a dollar per bottle."

—Pitcher to Dragons

PRODUCT DESCRIPTION

A self-serve laundry detergent vending machine.

DRAGONS' DEN BY THE NUMBERS

- **The Ask:** $500,000 for 40% equity in the company
- **Company Valuation:** $1,250,000
- **The Deal:** $0
- **25:** The number of bottles sold per machine per week
- **15:** The number of seconds that it takes to refill your bottle with laundry detergent
- **12:** The number of weeks that the pitcher's machines have been in use
- **100:** The number of new machines the company will build if they receive investor funding

Pitcher Martin Gagne of Dans un Jardin demonstrating his eco-friendly laundry detergent vending machine.

THE WARM-UP: BUSINESS PLAN DEFINED

A **business plan** is a 10- to 40-page document that outlines your strategy for each segment of your business, including your product or service, business model, sales and marketing strategy, team, and financing. The purpose of a business plan is to:

- **Define Strategy:** To describe the tactics and the product, marketing, financial, and operational strategies that you will employ to capture a definable market.
- **Secure Funding:** To describe how you plan to achieve the financial objectives of each of the stakeholders in your business (investors, customers, founders, employees).

BUSINESS PLAN TABLE OF CONTENTS

There is no set format for a business plan, only similar talking points and categories that are used across business plan formats. Use this book to answer the critical strategy questions of your business, then format your notes using the method in this book, or bring in an outside adviser to do so.

The following is a sample table of contents for a business plan. Once you complete your business plan, be prepared to customize it for banks or investors as required.

TITLE PAGE
- Company Name and Logo
- Contact Information
- Business Plan Copy Number

TABLE OF CONTENTS PAGE

EXECUTIVE SUMMARY SECTION (see Chapter 8)

1. VISION, MISSION, GOALS SECTION (see Chapter 11)
    A. Business Description
    B. Vision and Mission

    C. Business Objectives

    D. Milestones

    E. Business History

2. **PRODUCT/SERVICE DESCRIPTION SECTION** (see Chapter 12)

    A. Customer Problem

    B. Product/Service Description

    C. Core Features and Benefits

    D. Proprietary Assets

    E. Product Lifecycle

    F. Product Roadmap

3. **MARKET DEFINITION SECTION** (see Chapter 13)

    A. Market Opportunity

    B. Target-Market Profile

    C. Growth Strategy

4. **COMPETITIVE ANALYSIS SECTION** (see Chapter 14)

    A. Competition

    B. Competitive Advantage

    C. Barriers to Entry

5. **BUSINESS MODEL SECTION** (see Chapter 15)

    A. Value Chain

    B. Product/Market Fit

    C. Revenue Model

    D. Scalability

6. **SALES AND MARKETING STRATEGY SECTION** (see Chapter 16)

    A. Positioning

    B. Pricing Strategy

    C. Sales Strategy

    D. Marketing Strategy

    E. Strategic Relationships

    F. Sales Forecast

7. **MANAGEMENT AND ORGANIZATION SECTION** (see Chapter 17)
   A. Business Organization
   B. Management Team
   C. Advisory Board
   D. Professional Support
   E. Hiring Needs

8. **FINANCIAL PLAN SECTION** (see Chapter 18)
   A. Financial Summary
   B. Financing Details
   C. Financial Performance
   D. Risk and Mitigation

SUPPORTING DOCUMENTS

In addition to a core business plan document, a bank or investor might ask you for some or all of the following supporting documents.

- Monthly profit and loss statement, cash-flow statement, balance sheet
- Manager bios or resumés
- Legal documents (patents, intellectual property, contracts, distribution agreements, etc.)
- Product or service diagrams or flow charts.
- Personal financial statements (upon request)
- Operations plan (see Chapter 19 to learn how to build this stand-alone document)

DRAGON LORE

Put more effort into the *business-planning* process than into the *business plan formatting* process. If you are not a writer, hire someone to format your notes into a proper business-planning document.

Back in 1996, two entrepreneurs, Larry Finnson and Chris Emery, launched an idea for a business based on a product that Chris's grandmother had made as a treat: Clodhoppers fudge-covered graham clusters. Ten years later, their Clodhoppers brand was sold to another company, Brookside, leaving the friends without a business to run. So they returned to their chocolate-making roots and came up with a completely new brand called OMG's, which they brought into the Dragons' Den. Their experience and expertise meant that they had a relatively easy time there, and secured a deal.

OMG'S CANDY

Pitchers: Larry Finnson and Chris Emery, Season 6, Episode 16

BUSINESS MODEL

The business produces and markets a line of super-premium chocolate products that they sell through retailers.

PROBLEM

How to replicate the commercial success of their first product, Clodhoppers.

SOLUTION

Develop and sell a new product: chocolate graham wafer clusters mixed with gourmet nuts and crunchy toffee bits. The product comes in dark, white, and milk chocolate flavours.

GO-TO-MARKET

The pitchers plan to start selling through specialty retailers in Year 1, and transition to mainstream retailers in Year 2; Years 5 to 7 will entail retailing everywhere candy is sold in Canada.

TEAM

Larry Finnson and Chris Emery have been in the candy industry since 1996, when their famous Clodhoppers product was launched.

FINANCIALS

The Ask: $250,000 for 30% equity in the company
Company Valuation: $833,333

Current Year Revenue: $0
The Deal: $250,000 for 50% equity in the business

Pitchers Larry Finnson and Chris Emery from OMG's Candy handing out their OMG's chocolate clusters to the Dragons.

SELF-STUDY WORKSHOP: Business Plan Pre-Work

Use the section-by-section workshops in the following eight chapters to answer critical questions about your business. Then format your answers into the business plan format (Business Plan Table of Contents) provided in this chapter, or use the format that your investor or bank requests.

1. Your Audience: For **whom** are you creating your business?
    - ❑ **Yourself, friends and family, individual investors:** Use the workshops in this book to develop your business plan talking points. Use the format in this book to produce your plan.
    - ❑ **Investor groups, banks, business competitions:** Use the workshops in this book to develop your business plan talking points. Then format your plan using the template that is required by the organization.

2. How experienced are you at using **computer sofware**?
    - ❑ Experienced
    - ❑ Not experienced (if not, find help)

3. How comfortable are you at putting together **financial statements**?
    - ❑ Comfortable
    - ❑ Not comfortable (if not, find help)

4. What types **of advisers** do you have access to?
   - ❑ Chartered accountant (who can help you put together your financial statements)
   - ❑ Business consultant (who can help you refine the business plan talking points that you have created)
   - ❑ Lawyer (who can help you review the legal feasibility and regulatory requirements of your business model)
   - ❑ Writer (who can help you format the business plan talking points that you have created in this book into a business plan)

In this chapter we outlined the eight core sections of a business plan. In the next eight chapters, you'll work through eight workshops to complete your business plan. No business plan can be completed in one session, so be sure to complete and refine your strategy over time until you have a winning business plan.

PART III

How to Build a Business Plan

Describe your business model, vision, mission, goals, and strategies.

CHAPTER 11

WHAT IS YOUR VISION FOR YOUR BUSINESS?

"You've got to be careful who you take as an investor. You need people who are going to listen to you, and work with you . . . not just chirp at you."
—Dragon to Pitcher

SECTION 1: VISION, MISSION, GOALS

Explain your vision for your business. Clarify your mission, business objectives, and critical milestones. Recap your business history.

Back in 1963, Mary Kay Ash used $5,000 in savings to start a business selling something she loved.[1] But her big idea wasn't just a product, it was an entire business model built around helping women start businesses with a small minimum investment. Using the experience she gained while working for Stanley Home Products, she taught women to go to market with her Mary Kay cosmetics line by doing business with friends and family, holding weekly appointments, and teaching free skin care classes. In her version of a free sampling program (where something is offered for free in order to entice customers into buying the product) free skin care classes were offered to prospective customers, who were then encouraged to buy her cosmetics. Each rep tapped into her own circle of influence, armed with kits that would help her do facials for women at her friends' homes. The more facials that reps gave away, the more cosmetics they sold. Today, anyone can become an independent sales rep for the Mary Kay line after a small initial investment. The revenue model? Reps who retail the product keep 50% commission against the suggested retail price, and Mary Kay Inc. keeps the rest. Today Mary Kay Inc. boasts over 2 million independent sales reps worldwide.

All businesses start with a product or service and an entrepreneurial dream, and Mary Kay Ash's vision was a cosmetics empire that empowered women to start their own businesses. The ability to communicate that vision and show how a product or service fills a market void or solves a real problem will make a business plan much more attractive to investors and customers. When Sarah Doherty of SideStix Ventures Inc.'s forearm crutches visited the Dragons' Den, the fact that she had only sold 50 crutches the previous year didn't hold back the investors. Her personal story and her ability to communicate her vision overrode any question of whether she had a real business or not.

SIDESTIX VENTURES INC.

Pitchers: Sarah Doherty and Kerith Perreur-Lloyd, Season 6, Episode 9

Focus: Communicate Your Vision

> "At age 13 I lost my leg to a drunk driver, but I was determined not to lose my freedom. I began to adapt forearm crutches, which enabled me to become the first amputee to summit Mount McKinley . . . And there's no way I could've done it on [regular crutches]. It just caused a lot of pain. It caused chafing under my arms. These have been designed specifically . . . we have a leather pad to prevent bruising and chafing. We have angles that put your hands in the best position for weight lifting. Our grips are contoured and padded just like a running shoe. We have a dampening shock absorber to take away the bumps and jolts."
> —Pitcher to Dragons

PRODUCT DESCRIPTION

Forearm crutches made of super-light carbon fibre.

DRAGONS' DEN BY THE NUMBERS

- **The Ask:** $60,000 for 20% of the business
- **Company Valuation:** $300,000
- **The Deal:** $60,000 for 30% of the business
- **$32,000:** Sales last year
- **$30,000:** Proportion of the capital they will use to produce inventory
- **50:** The number of pairs of crutches that they sold last year

Sarah Doherty and Kerith Perreur-Lloyd pitching their SideStix.

SECTION 1: VISION, MISSION, GOALS

The vision, mission, goals section of your business plan is a declarative statement that summarizes your vision for your business, including your business structure, mission statement, financial and non-financial objectives and milestones, and company history. It's an important opening section for your business plan because it gives the investor your backstory and explains why you are in business. It should be succinct, motivational, and time bound. It should be relevant to all stakeholders, including investors, company founders, customers, and employees, as well as to the business environment in which you work. And it should tell the reader what milestones you have achieved to date. In this section of your business plan, include the following subsections:

A. **Business Description:** What your business does, and the legal structure you have established.
B. **Vision and Mission:** Why you are in business, and what your business will look like in the future.
C. **Business Objectives:** Financial and non-financial goals for your business.
D. **Milestones:** Specific projects you expect to complete by certain deadlines.
E. **Business History:** What your business has achieved to date.

A. Business Description

In this section of your business plan, describe what your business is, what it does, when you started, and what type of legal structure you have established. This should be just a brief overview of your business in two to three sentences.

B. Vision and Mission

The single most effective way to stay motivated, even when faced with your deepest challenges, is to remember why the world is better off with your business than it is without it. A mission statement is a declarative statement of the marketplace void that you fill. The following are some examples of high-profile mission statements:

- **Google:** To organize the world's information and make it universally accessible and useful.
- **Microsoft:** To enable people and businesses throughout the world to realize their full potential.
- **Twitter:** To help you share and discover what's happening now among all the things, people, and events you care about.

The companion statement to a mission statement is the vision statement. Every business team needs something to strive for, and a vision statement is a declarative statement of what you want your business to be in the future. By stating your vision, and spreading the message to each of your stakeholders, you can create a singular focus for everyone who has a vested interest in your success. Here are some vision statement examples:

- To be the leader in upcycling of pre-consumer waste from consumer products within three years.
- To be the Microsoft of the bushing industry.
- To be the leading recycler of used cellphones in eastern Canada.
- To be the leading online retailer of refurbished children's toys.

C. Business Objectives

A mission statement won't do you any good if you can't stay in business. Business goals delineate what you want in return for your efforts. Knowing what your financial (revenue, profit, etc.) and non-financial (company size, location, etc.) business goals are in advance will help you keep your team on track. For each goal, set a specific time limit and make sure that it is powerful enough to keep you motivated, and realistic enough to be achievable.

D. Milestones

Investors like to have a clear understanding of how you will use their capital. While going through the business-planning process, you'll come up with a list of high-level projects that are necessary to achieve those goals. A milestone table should include the following elements:

- Key projects
- Expected completion dates
- Funding requirements

E. Business History

In this section, you should briefly summarize where you are in your business, and why you are writing your business plan. Most business plans are written to request funding from a bank or an investor. However, for someone with an established business whose sales have levelled off, a business plan can kick-start your business. Whatever your reason is for writing a business plan, state it very clearly so that the potential stakeholders who read it know what your call to action is.

DRAGON LORE

The driving force behind any business is the vision and mission of the entrepreneur.

No one said pitching to investors is a conflict-free process, and even if you have self-audited your business and have all of your legal, financial, and operational ducks in a row, some investors just might not be interested in your venture. When pitchers Tony Hancock and David Damberger from Ethical Ocean visited the Dragons' Den, they stepped into the crossfire and actually offended one of the Dragons. No surprise there—that's why we love the show. But when a debate raged over whether or not their ethical website business concept meant that the rest of the consumer-goods world was *not* ethical, the pitchers stood their ground. They remained calm, and they walked away with a deal.

ETHICAL OCEAN

Pitchers: Tony Hancock and David Damberger, Season 5, Episode 20

BUSINESS MODEL

The company makes money charging vendors of ethical products a 12% commission to sell their merchandise through the Ethical Ocean website.

PROBLEM

If you want to buy fair-trade coffee, organic baby oil, or other fair-trade products, you have to go to three different stores.

SOLUTION

A one-stop online marketplace where vendors from across North America can upload their ethical products and sell directly to people who visit the site.

GO-TO-MARKET

The company started signing up vendors two months ago.

TEAM

The founders are Tony Hancock and David Damberger from Calgary. Both have a history of working for social change. Tony's experience includes working on an energy and biomass conservation program in Malawi.[2] David's experience includes working in India with vegetable-growing village cooperatives.[3]

FINANCIALS

The Ask: $150,000 for 20% equity in the company
Company Valuation: $750,000
Current-Year Revenue Projection: Not available
The Deal: $150,000 for 20% equity in the company

Tony Hancock and David Damberger pitching their online marketplace for ethical products.

SELF-STUDY WORKSHOP: Vision, Mission, Goals

For this section of your business plan, draft your talking points first by answering the relevant questions below. Then weave your answers together into a paragraph or two, bullet points when necessary, and tables or diagrams if appropriate for each of A, B, C, D, and E.

VISION, MISSION, GOALS

A. Business Description
B. Vision and Mission
C. Business Objectives
D. Milestones
E. Business History

A. BUSINESS DESCRIPTION

Background: What is the name of your company, and how long have you been in business?
Entity Type: What type of legal entity have you established, and how many owners are there?
Product or Service Sold: What product or service do you sell?
Customers Served: Who will buy/use your product or service?

Repeat Revenue Model: How will you generate repeat revenues annually? Will you produce and market your products yourself, or license them to others who pay you a transaction fee?

Plan Write-Up: *Weave your answers together into a paragraph, using bullet points when necessary.*

B. VISION AND MISSION

Vision: What will your business look like in three to five years? In what business category and geographic market will you be the leader?

Core Purpose: What is the highest and best use for your product or service? What problem does it solve? How does it improve people's lives? How does it help people?

Primary Market Served: What will be your primary target market?

Core Expertise: What capability makes your team uniquely qualified to solve this problem?

Plan Write-Up: *Weave your answers together into a paragraph, using bullet points when necessary.*

C. BUSINESS OBJECTIVES

Financial Objectives: What are your revenue, profit, and return on investment goals for the next three to five years?

Non-Financial Objectives: What are your non-financial business goals for the next three to five years (such as company size, location, new product lines)?

Plan Write-Up: *Weave your answers together into a paragraph, using bullet points when necessary.*

D. MILESTONES

What major marketing, product-development, or operational projects are you looking to complete in the next six months to three years?

Plan Write-Up: *Summarize your milestones.*

Major Projects Pending	Completion Date	Funding Required

E. BUSINESS HISTORY

How far along are you with your business? What stage of development are you in? Do you have a prototype, or is your concept just notes on a napkin? Why are you writing this business plan, and why do you really need the funding?

Why did you start the company? What prompted you to give up your day job and take a risk as an entrepreneur?

Plan Write-Up: Weave your answers together into a paragraph, using bullet points when necessary.

Having a clear vision, mission, and goals for your business will help you make better decisions and will help you create buy-in with your team. In this chapter, you created a basic description of your business and a clear set of milestones so that investors will have a clear picture of what you do, and why they should get involved. In the next chapter, you'll create a detailed product description that explains why your product or service is so compelling and what is proprietary about it.

CHAPTER 12

WHAT IS YOUR BIG IDEA?

"You know your stuff. You've done something very few people could ever do. It's amazing!"
—Dragon to Pitcher

SECTION 2: PRODUCT/SERVICE DESCRIPTION

State the most pressing problem that your product or service addresses. Describe your product or service, how it solves that problem, and why it is different from its competitors. Outline your roadmap for how your product or service will evolve over time.

Every great business plan should have an original idea, or it won't stand out in the minds of investors, customers, or other stakeholders. Your original idea can be something technical, economical, or service-oriented about your product or service. Or it can be a unique revenue or distribution model for what otherwise might seem like an unsellable product or service. If you don't already have an original idea, you might need to go through the entire business-concept-definition process again to find it. (Refer to *The Dragons' Den Guide to Assessing Your Business Concept*).

In the movie *A Beautiful Mind*, based on the life of John Nash, Nash (played by Russell Crowe) searches endlessly for an original idea that will ensure his legacy. When he finally finds it, the idea becomes known as the "Nash Equilibrium" and leads to a Nobel Prize in Economic Sciences. The movie makes it clear that Nash's work was worth the effort. In business, your original idea is a common theme that makes your product or service worth talking about—whether it's during a 15-second introduction to an investor by a friend, a 30-second pitch in an elevator, a 10-minute PowerPoint presentation, or a two-page executive summary that you email out. Regardless of the type of pitch you are making, your original idea should be clear and compelling. In this section of your business plan, describe the most compelling features of your product or service, and why people will be willing to pay you for your solution.

Now, you don't need a Nobel Prize–worthy idea to get the attention of the Dragons. But you do need a clearly defined product or service that is compelling, and you need to show how it can earn them money. When Mike Solomita from Cefaly visited the Dragons' Den, his product idea was so original that he secured a deal while making one Dragon feel better during the process. The product was a drug-free migraine headache treatment and prevention device that you wear on your head. The design of the product is so unique that it looks like something you would find on an episode of *Star Trek*.

CEFALY MIGRAINE DEVICE

Pitcher: Mike Solomita, Season 6, Episode 3

Focus: Define Your Idea

"The first ever [medical] device to be certified by Health Canada for the treatment and prevention of migraines without the use of drugs or medication. The device does a little bit of electrical stimulation on the brain and what that does is it actually creates endorphins and these endorphins then block out the pain receptors."
—Pitcher to Dragons

PRODUCT DESCRIPTION

A CE- and ISO-certified medical device designed to treat and prevent migraine headaches.

DRAGONS' DEN BY THE NUMBERS

- **The Ask:** $100,000 for 5% royalty
- **Company Valuation:** Not applicable because no equity has been offered (only a royalty has been offered).
- **The Deal:** $100,000 in exchange for 25% royalty until capital is returned, followed by a 10% royalty thereafter
- **30,000:** The approximate number of units that have been sold in Europe
- **$299:** The retail price for the Cefaly
- **80%:** The percentage of the funding that will be spent on marketing

Mike Solomita pitching the Cefaly.

SECTION 2: PRODUCT/SERVICE DESCRIPTION

The product/service description section of your business plan is a detailed explanation of how your product or service works, and why it is unique. The purpose of a product description is to communicate how it solves a customer problem and why there is a real need for it in the marketplace. This section of your business plan should include the following subsections:

A. **Customer Problem:** The problem or gap in the market that caused you to get into the market.
B. **Product/Service Description:** What you are selling.
C. **Core Features and Benefits:** What it is about your product or service that stands out, and why it is important.
D. **Proprietary Assets:** What type of intellectual property or proprietary agreements you have in place to fend off copycat competitors.
E. **Product Lifecycle:** What stage of the product lifecycle your product or service category is in.
F. **Product Roadmap:** How your product or product line/service will evolve over time.

A. Customer Problem and B. Product Description

A problem statement is a description of the issue that the customer will pay you to solve. It can be an economic, technical, or social problem, or it can just be a void that you are filling because no other solution exists. In these first two sections of your product description, clearly communicate what your product or service is, how it works to solve a problem, and why it is original in some way. Also discuss how people currently solve the problem. If you want to improve the way you describe your product or service, try setting up an informal focus group of potential customers, and ask them to describe what you sell. Sometimes someone other than you will be better at describing your offering.

C. Core Features and Benefits

In this section of your business plan, briefly describe the components of your product or service that make it special. Also describe why each component is valuable. For example, while a key feature of an environmentally friendly pen might be that it is made of biodegradable materials, the key benefits of your pen might be that it writes as well as any other pen, costs less, and doesn't hurt the environment. A key feature of a restaurant menu might be that it contains buffalo burgers, and a relevant benefit of the restaurant menu might be that buffalo burgers are healthier than, and cost the same as, beef burgers.

The features to list in your business plan are the ones that solve relevant customer problems and that people are willing to pay you for. Discussing features that are provided by most alternative solutions serve little or no purpose to the reader of your plan. For each feature that you describe, be sure to mention what that feature does and what it means to the customer. For example, Kleenex Anti-Viral tissue has a specially treated middle layer, which means the tissue kills 99.9% of cold and flu viruses in the tissue. A service feature of FedEx is dependable, timely delivery, which means you'll know exactly what time your package will arrive before, and will therefore be less stressed while you wait for delivery.

Here is a brief description of the types of benefits you should touch on for each of the core features of your product or service:

- **Rational Benefits:** A rational benefit describes the quantifiable value of your product or service. This may include the basic function of your product or service. For example, your car transports you to work, your stove cooks your food, and your lawn-care service removes weeds from your grass. A rational benefit also includes the monetary value of your product or service. When describing this value, be specific. For example, if your product cuts homeowners' heating bills, try to quantify that monetary savings. Or if your product helps people make money, describe how much.

- **Emotional Benefits:** Emotional benefits are less quantifiable. For example, many people buy cars that reflect how they feel about themselves or what they aspire to. Most stoves can get the job done, but some people pay extra for a stove that is visually appealing. And while your lawn-care service removes weeds from your grass, many people like the improved look of their lawn when it is cared for professionally.
- **Social Benefits (Hybrid):** Social benefits provide both rational and emotional benefits. Social consciousness is good for the environment (a rational benefit) and makes people feel good (an emotional benefit). To communicate social benefits, describe how your product or service is eco-friendly, adheres to fair-trade practices, promotes social change, or anything else that relates to social consciousness. If your product makes your company a triple bottom line business with people, planet, and profit at the core of your business philosophy, this is where you should say it.

D. Proprietary Assets

It's important for investors to know that competitors won't be able to readily copy your hard work. Many features of your product or service simply can't be safeguarded, but intellectual property (IP) is an asset that can be protected from unauthorized use. The following table shows the types of intellectual property protection available to you. Always speak with a lawyer to ensure that you have the level of protection that your product or service needs or is entitled to. The rules relating to what is patentable are very complex and depend upon the market segment your product is in. Other protection, like non-compete contracts, may have more moral than legal suasion in the end result, and also have standard rules of thumb that you should be aware of. In this section of your business plan, discuss any IP protection that you have, or could have in place at some point in the future.

TYPES OF LEGAL PROTECTION*

What Can Be Protected?	What Can Be Protected?	Term of Protection*
Authored works such as drawings, software programs, books, articles, or music.	Copyright	Life of the author plus 50 years.
Inventions such as equipment or processes.	Patents	Up to 20 years.

(*Continued*)

What Can Be Protected?	What Can Be Protected?	Term of Protection*
Symbols, names, and logos that you use to identify your product or service.	Trademarks	Potentially indefinitely.
Trade secrets: formulas or processes that you keep a secret.	Non-disclosure agreements (a.k.a. confidentiality agreements)	For as long as you or your employees don't leak it to the public.
Contracts with your employees to keep them from setting up shop with the same business idea after they leave your company.	Non-compete agreements	Depends on the locality.

*Always speak to a lawyer to clarify your rights in Canada and other countries.

E. Product Lifecycle

When an innovative product, such as a tablet computer or an e-book reader, is first introduced to the market, it has few, if any, competitors. Over time, however, competitors sense profit and enter the market with their own version of the product. Eventually many different brands are on the market, with many different feature sets. Over time, those feature sets become somewhat standardized, and at that point the product or service category has entered the maturity phase. The product or service category then either settles into a mature market, with few if any *new* competitors. Or it moves into decline, and maybe even disappears, like the typewriter. This series of changes is called the product lifecycle. Understanding where your product or service fits into the lifecycle will help you to determine the types of strategies you can adopt to compete.

In this section of your business plan, describe the lifecycle stage that your product or service is in. The following are the four core stages in the product lifecycle:

THE PRODUCT LIFECYCLE

Introduction	Growth	Maturity	Decline
A product or service type that very few people have ever seen. Much of your time will be spent demonstrating how your product or service works to solve a customer problem.	A product or service category that is starting to catch on with the public, but many people still have not tried it. Your time will be spent educating the public and differentiating your product or service features.	A product or service category that is well-known and somewhat saturated with competitors. Much of your time will be spent marketing your brand through consistent advertising and promotional efforts.	A product or service category that is disappearing because innovations are rapidly displacing the category. Much of your time will be spent in price wars with other discounters.

F. Product Roadmap

When a product or service becomes profitable, it attracts competition. In order to continue to maintain distance between your offering and that of the competition, ongoing improvement projects must be budgeted for in your financial plan. That's where a product roadmap comes in. A product roadmap is a list of line extensions, feature improvements to your current offerings, or even planned obsolescence of your current offerings over time.

Your roadmap (a.k.a. research and development) budget should be commensurate with the type of industry you are in. Software companies, for example, must constantly develop and release new iterations of their product based on operating-system changes and feedback from their users. Other product or service roadmaps may be as simple as a plan to test new menu items for your restaurant, or to add new services to your lawn-care business in the future. A roadmap can even include new product ideas if you are an upcycling business, or testing new raw materials if you are trying to come up with a replacement for a children's toy box.

In this section of your business plan, include a summary of how your product or service will evolve over time.

DRAGON LORE

A product is not a business. To turn a product into a business, you need a way to generate repeat revenue from each customer.

The products and services that are easiest to explain are the ones that eliminate pain or solve a problem. When your product or service addresses pain, it becomes easy to demonstrate in front of a live customer. Unless, of course, you have to drink to excess to make it work, and you don't have time to take your prospective customer to a bar. Knowing that his time was limited, pitcher Bradley Friesen from LastCall decided to bring an award-winning bartender with him on the show as well as a stocked bar so any willing Dragons could experience the value of his product first-hand. His "solution"? A hangover-prevention beverage called LastCall.

LASTCALL

Pitcher: Bradley Friesen, Season 6, Episode 20

BUSINESS MODEL

Sales of a patented cap and bottle and a proprietary beverage mixture that prevents hangovers. The patented cap-and-bottle delivery system also has the potential for licensing for other beverage products and uses.

PROBLEM

How to relieve hangover symptoms.

SOLUTION

A functional beverage called LastCall that you consume as the last drink of the night to prevent the symptoms of a hangover. The beverage is delivered in a patented cap-and-bottle system, whereby powder is stored in the bottle cap until the cap is twisted, at which point the powder is delivered into the water in the bottle. The powder releases melatonin, dehydrated ginger, and vitamins B and C, which all work together to prevent a hangover.

GO-TO-MARKET

Friesen plans to sell LastCall through bars and nightclubs.

TEAM

Bradley Friesen worked in the plastics business in injection moulding until he was laid off a year ago. He devoted the past year to coming up with the cure for the common hangover.

FINANCIALS

> **The Ask:** $5,000 for 5% equity in the company
> **Company Valuation:** $100,000
> **Current-Year Revenue Projection:** Not given
> **The Deal:** $25,000 for 10% of the company from all five Dragons

Bradley Friesen pitching a functional beverage called LastCall that helps prevent hangovers.

SELF-STUDY WORKSHOP: Product/Service Description

For this section of your business plan, draft your talking points first by answering the relevant questions below. Then weave your answers together into a paragraph or two, bullet points when necessary, and tables or diagrams if appropriate for each of A, B, C, D, E, and F.

SECTION 2: PRODUCT/SERVICE DESCRIPTION

A. Customer Problem
B. Product/Service Description
C. Core Features and Benefits
D. Proprietary Assets
E. Product Lifecycle
F. Product Roadmap

A. CUSTOMER PROBLEM

Plan Write-Up: Summarize your customer problem.

B. PRODUCT/SERVICE DESCRIPTION

Product Description: Describe your product.
Operational Concept: How does it work?
Product Environment: Where will your product be consumed or service performed?

Competitive Products: What types of products or services currently compete with yours?

Plan Write-Up: Weave your answers together into a paragraph, using bullet points when necessary.

C. CORE FEATURES AND BENEFITS

Positioning: Finish this sentence: "Our product/service is the only one that . . ."

Features: What are two to three unique components of your product or service offering, and why are they important?

Attributes: How is your product or service faster, more convenient, or higher performing than alternative offerings on the market?

Benefits: What is the rational value (functional or monetary benefit) of your product or service? What is the emotional value of your product or service? What social value does your product or service provide?

After-Sales Support: After the customer buys from you, what type of ongoing support do you provide for your product or service?

Plan Write-Up: Weave your answers together into a paragraph, using bullet points when necessary.

D. PROPRIETARY ASSETS

What are the proprietary features of your product or service (trademarks, patents, copyrights, licensing agreements, etc.)?

Plan Write-Up: Summarize your proprietary assets.

E. PRODUCT LIFECYCLE

Plan Write-Up: Summarize the product-lifecycle stage that you are in.

F. PRODUCT ROADMAP

Feature Rollout: What features will you roll out over time?

Line Extensions: What related products or services could you launch in the future?

Plan Write-Up: Summarize your product roadmap.

A product or service with an original idea or a "wow" factor is a core element of a sustainable business model and an attractive business plan. In the next chapter, you'll determine the market opportunity, the customers you will target, and the market dynamics that support your business model.

CHAPTER 13

HOW BIG IS THE MARKET?

"They know what we want to hear, know what they want to do when they get there. The country's in great shape when you see this coming."
    —Dragon to Pitcher

SECTION 3: MARKET DEFINITION

Describe your ideal customer. Estimate the total dollar amount that your target market will collectively spend on products or services like yours. Outline your growth strategy.

If Einstein were using the scientific method to start a business, he'd probably do a lot of research first. He might start by *observing* an unsolved customer problem or gap in the market. Then he'd carefully craft a *hypothesis* for a product or service that could solve that problem. Next, he'd set up an *experiment* using a prototype and a test market to see if his proposed solution was feasible. And, finally, he'd come to a *conclusion* as to whether or not his business idea was commercially viable. He'd use the scientific method because it works, whether you are undertaking a scientific experiment or starting a business. And by doing so, he'd acknowledge that every business is an experiment until proven otherwise.

Market research can help you through this experimental process. Prototypes and go-to-market strategies cost money. Pilot tests consume resources. And business start-ups can leave you personally bankrupt if you don't do your homework. The fact is, every time you have to go back to the drawing board, you burn through resources, and you might not have enough funding in place to weather the storm of repeated failures. Your best hope is to increase the odds of success by completing a feasibility study and a thorough analysis of the size of your market opportunity before you open your doors for business.

Pitchers Pierre Beaupre and Jean-Daniel Nieminen of Flush₂O came into the Dragon's Den with lots of research about the market for their product—an environmentally friendly retrofit for toilets that regulates the amount of water you use on each flush. They knew their technology and they have taken prototypes to trade shows where they have generated a lot of interest in their product. The only thing they didn't have was sales! For some Dragons, that was enough to put the deal on ice, but one Dragon could see the potential, and was willing to invest to help them get to market.

FLUSH₂O

Pitchers: Pierre Beaupre and Jean-Daniel Nieminen, Season 5, Episode 19

Focus: Define Your Market

> "Toilets in North America are flushed [using] drinkable water. That's a lot of waste of good water. I invented a dual-flush retrofitsystem that converts any existing toilet into a dual-flush toilet without any tool or the need of a plumber."
> —Pitcher to Dragons

PRODUCT DESCRIPTION

An environmentally friendly dual-flush retrofit system for toilets.

DRAGONS' DEN BY THE NUMBERS

- **The Ask:** $125,000 for 15% of the business
- **Company Valuation:** $833,000
- **The Deal:** $125,000 for 50% of the company
- **$0:** Sales to date
- **$100,000:** How much the pitchers have invested to date
- **$20:** Retail price for the product
- **200 million:** The approximate number of toilets in residences in North America.

Pitchers Pierre Beaupre and Jean-Daniel Nieminen with Flush$_2$o.

SECTION 3: MARKET DEFINITION

The market definition section of your business plan describes the customers who will buy from you, the size of the market for your type of product or service, and the market share that you expect to achieve. The purpose of this section of your business plan is to show that your business is commercially viable and that the market is sizable enough to warrant investment. This section of your business plan should include the following subsections:

A. **Market Opportunity:** Market size, industry drivers, and trends.
B. **Target-Market Profile:** Target-market profiles, and motivation for buying.
C. **Growth Strategy:** Potential markets you could target in the future.

A. Market Opportunity

Market Analysis

One of the most rewarding aspects of the business-planning process is market research. You can use it to uncover industry secrets, competitor weaknesses, and new markets that you never knew you had. The process involves both primary and secondary sources of information. Primary sources include direct conversations with, or analysis of, customers, suppliers, industry associations, and even competitors. Secondary sources of information refer to market or industry research completed by others. You should use a combination of both in your business plan. In this part of your business plan, try to discuss the following elements:

- **Key Players:** Refer to the two or three dominant businesses in your industry, which you are trying to compete with or displace.

- **Trends:** Refer to the patterns of success that have emerged in your industry that support your business plan. These include social, economic, technological, or regulatory trends. They can even refer to a wave of product or service innovations, new product design features, or new categories of service.
- **Cyclicality:** Refers to the way your revenue will rise or fall with the peaks and troughs of the business cycle.
- **Seasonality:** Refers to the way your revenue will rise or fall based on the seasons of the year (winter, spring, summer, fall).
- **Compound Annual Growth Rate (CAGR):** Refers to the growth rate of similar businesses in your industry or of the industry itself. These figures will later provide backup to your sales forecast.

Market Size

Given the amount of time and resources that you are planning to risk on your business venture, it's important to make sure that your target market is sizable enough to justify the effort. Your market also must be readily identifiable and easily accessible, or you'll have a difficult time coming up with an efficient sales and marketing strategy. Calculating the size of your product or service's market is not an easy task, and is a purely hypothetical process at best. But it is an important exercise to go through because it will give you a general idea of the volume of sales you might achieve based on the market share you expect to capture. Estimates like these give you a target to shoot for, not an exact prediction of what your revenues will be. In this section of your business plan, include an estimate of the number of potential customers there are for your category of product or service, as well as a projected dollar volume of sales for that category. There are two approaches you can use to do this rough calculation:

- **Top-Down Approach:** Research the total industry-wide sales volume for your category of product or service. Find this information through your industry association, or through the information sources provided later in this chapter.
- **Bottom-Up Approach:** Conduct primary research with businesses in your industry to estimate the number of potential customers in your geographic market who may use your category of product or service.

B. Target-Market Profile

Who are the potential customers for your product or service, what are their needs, and how big is each potential target group? The total market for your type of product or service can be segmented into a number of homogeneous customer groups. For example, if you sell waterless car-wash products, you can segment the market by luxury-car owners, high school fundraising committees, and truck drivers. How you come up with those segments is up to you. You can undertake in-depth research into your industry using the sources mentioned earlier. You can brainstorm a list in your garage and add to it over time. Or you can do a combination of both. When you describe how the market for your product or service is segmented, try to consider each customer group using the following profiles:

- **Geographic Profile (Where They Are):** Where are your likely customers concentrated geographically? Are they restricted to a city, province, or country? Defining where your customers are concentrated can help you determine where to advertise and where to send your sales force.
- **Demographic Profile (Who They Are):** What are the average age, income, education, family size, and occupation of your likely customer? Demographic information is readily available (see pages 130–132), so deciding on a profile in advance can help you find those typical customers.
- **Psychographic Profile (How They Are):** What are their personalities like? Are they easygoing, pessimistic, or passionate? Or do they have some other recognizable personality trait that is relevant to your product offering?
- **Behavioural Profile (What They Do):** What type of work, sports, or hobbies do your ideal customers do? Defining the lifestyle and personality traits of your ideal customers can further help to root out those customers who will bring you the most profit and to refine your product or service to meet their requirements.

Buying Motives

Two customers might buy exactly the same product for completely different reasons. For example, one person might buy a coffee to wake up, while another might buy a coffee for pleasure while socializing. One person might buy a computer to do work, while another might buy one to play video games. And one person might buy a watch to tell time, while another might buy a watch to track running times or to impress a date. Understanding the motives behind your customers' purchasing habits will help you produce marketing and communications materials that resonate with your target audience.

Buying motives include the following:

- **Rational Motives:** A customer's need to solve a specific problem or address a specific issue.
- **Monetary Motives:** A customer's need to cut costs, increase revenue, improve profit, or save time.
- **Productivity Motives:** A customer's need to increase output.
- **Emotional Motives:** A customer's desire to achieve peace of mind, feel better, etc.
- **Social Motives:** A customer's desire to sustain the earth by purchasing eco-friendly products that promote social change or adhere to fair-trade practices, for example.

C. Growth Strategy

Growth opportunities come from many sources, including acquisitions, joint ventures, untapped markets, or new products (or services). You can sell new products to current markets. You can sell current products to new markets. Or you can sell new products to new markets. You can do this on your own or with strategic partners. In this section of your business plan, describe how you plan to grow:

- **Current Markets:** Increase usage among current customers.
- **New Markets:** Come up with new applications for your product or service so that it appeals to new markets.
- **New Products**: Sell new products to current or new markets.

Where to Find the Information to Conduct Market Research

You can save yourself years of trouble by researching your industry before you commit major resources to your new business. In North America, each industry has a North American Industry Classification System (NAICS) code (formerly known as a Standard Industrial Classification, or SIC, code), which you can use to conduct online research or to buy an industry report from a firm that has already researched your market. To get started, look up your industry's code at www.naics.com.

Top Three Industry Information Sources

1. **Industry Trade Associations:** The first place to start your research is with your industry's trade association. A trade association is a membership organization that is funded by companies operating in the same line of business. It holds annual conferences, conducts research among members, and publishes the data it collects and makes it available for a fee (or sometimes free to members). You may have to join the association to access its information, but the few-hundred-dollar annual fee will definitely be worth it. And you might even find that continuing your membership on an annual basis will be good for your business.

2. **Industry Participants:** If you attend an annual conference or trade show, you can speak directly with a large number of industry vendors and participants who are often more than willing to share information. You can also contact your local chamber of commerce, which can provide local data if you are starting a business in the area.

3. **Online Search Engines:** The single most powerful source of data on your industry might just be the Internet. Just be sure to cross-reference your data so that you know you are dealing with fresh information. The great thing about search engines like Google or Bing is that you can explore for hours and find all kinds of market information. The problem with these search engines is that not all of the statistics found are real, relevant, or current. By cross-referencing your data against other sources of information, you'll be able to get a handle on which data you can trust, and which data you should ignore.

Other Sources of Information

- **Statistics Canada:** You can source vast amounts of demographic and economic data online through www.statcan.gc.ca, or the U.S. Census Bureau at www.census.gov if you are selling in the United States. This data can be used to support your decisions about business location, to assess traffic patterns for a retail outlet, or to determine future business needs based on the age of the population, for example.

- **Annual Reports:** Other rich sources of information are the annual reports filed by public companies. These companies are legally required to publish an annual report, which will often contain an industry outlook. You can get these reports for free by looking online at company websites, visiting databases that publish them (such as www.annualreports.com), or by contacting an investment broker. For example, if you are launching a cosmetics product, you could visit www.annualreports.com to review Revlon's annual report, which Revlon is required by the U.S. Securities and Exchange Commission to publish, to glean information about the industry. If you are launching a chocolate company, you could review The Hershey Company's annual report and learn about the market dynamics of its business.

- **Industry Research Firms:** Websites such as www.firstresearch.com (run by Hoover's), www.ibisworld.com, www.marketresearch.com, and www.bizminer.com can provide you with industry descriptions of just about any industry. These fee-based services provide high-level reviews of industries, so you'll have to dig down deep elsewhere if you want specific market-segment data and success factors. The cost per industry report can range from just over a hundred dollars to several thousand.

DRAGON LORE

If you spend too much time researching your market, then your market might pass you by. Sometimes it's better to go into a market 80% prepared, than to risk losing your market because you spent too much time doing research.

In many cases, the market for a product or service starts with you as the first customer. When the founders of HomeSav wanted to furnish their own homes, they found it difficult first to find the time to shop around, and second to find brand-name products at affordable prices. So they started a service that would help young professionals just like themselves.

HOMESAV

Pitchers: Allan Fisch, Aliza Pulver, and Alex Norman, Season 6, Episode 20

BUSINESS MODEL

Every day, the company posts on its website new sale items for which it has negotiated deep-discount prices. When a customer orders through the HomeSav website, the company puts through a purchase order to the manufacturer. The manufacturer gets the advantage of a wider potential market through the membership base of HomeSav. HomeSav never has the risk of holding inventory of any of the products it sells.

PROBLEM

How to find brand-name home decor you like at the price you can afford from the convenience of your home.

SOLUTION

A website that offers brand-name home decor at up to 70% off retail prices, delivered right to your door. Members sign up for free to receive access to exclusive deals.

GO-TO-MARKET

Uses a 45,000-user membership base of young professionals and the promise of branding and promotion to convince manufacturers to offer deep discounts on www.homesav.com.

TEAM

Allan Fisch has private equity experience and furniture industry experience. Aliza Pulver has worked as a lawyer, but also co-founded and acted as a buyer for two successful businesses. Alex Norman has investment banking experience, as well as consulting experience in marketing.

FINANCIALS

The Ask: $200,000 for 15% equity in the company
Company Valuation: $1.33 million
Current-Year Revenue Projection: $720,000
The Deal: $200,000 for 45% of the business

The team from HomeSav pitching their deep-discount home decor website to the Dragons.

SELF-STUDY WORKSHOP: Market Definition

For this section of your business plan, draft your talking points first by answering the relevant questions below. Then weave your answers together into a paragraph or two, using bullet points when necessary, and tables or diagrams if appropriate for each of A, B, and C. Try to answer as many questions as you can, but don't be alarmed if you can't answer all of these questions in one sitting. Market research takes time.

MARKET DEFINITION

A. Market Opportunity
B. Target-Market Profile
C. Growth Strategy

A. MARKET OPPORTUNITY

Market Need: Why does the market need a product or service like yours?

Industry: What industry are you operating in? What is the total market size for your type of product or service in the geographic market space you will compete in? What is the compound annual growth rate of your industry?

Demand Drivers: What drives demand in your industry? Is it product design, low price, a service option, or some other basis for competition?

Major Players: Who are the two or three major players in your industry?

Industry Trends: What industry trends support your business opportunity?

Business-Cycle Sensitivity: How sensitive is your industry to the changing of the business cycle and/or the changing of the seasons?

Plan Write-Up: *Weave your answers together into a paragraph, using bullet points to break up dense information.*

B. TARGET-MARKET PROFILE

Target Markets: What are your top three target markets?

Rational Needs: What rational motive will customers in your target markets have for buying your product/service, and how will your product/service meet this need? For example, *Our plumbing product plugs water leaks*.

Emotional Needs: What emotional motive will your customers have for buying your product/service, and how will your product/service meet this need? For example, *Our security feature gives the customer peace of mind*.

Social Needs: What social motives will your customers have for buying your product/service, and how will your product/service meet this need? For example, *We only use suppliers that adhere to fair-trade practices.*

Productivity Needs: What productivity motives will your customers have for buying your product/service, and how will your product/service meet this need? For example, *Our rice maker helps chefs cook twice the rice in half the time.*

Economic Needs: What economic motives will your customers have for buying your product/service, and how will your product/service meet this need? For example, *Our sensors detect energy loss, and with repairs, homeowners can cut down on their electricity bills.*

PRIMARY TARGET MARKET	Description
1. Demographic Profile (age/income/education level/ household size/occupation/gender)	
2. Geographic Profile (neighbourhood/city/county/region/province or state/nation/other)	
3. Behavioural Profile (associations/memberships/purchase habits)	
4. Customer Profile Give this target market a one- or two-word label, and then link the four profile descriptions into a single statement.	
SECONDARY TARGET MARKET	Description
1. Demographic Profile (age/income/education level/ household size/occupation/gender)	
2. Geographic Profile (neighbourhood/city/county/region/province or state/nation/other)	
3. Behavioural Profile (associations/memberships/purchase habits)	
4. Customer Profile Give this target market a one- or two-word label, and then link the four profile descriptions into a single statement.	

(Continued)

TERTIARY TARGET MARKET	Description
1. Demographic Profile (age/income/education level/ household size/occupation/gender)	
2. Geographic Profile (neighbourhood/city/county/region/province or state/nation/other)	
3. Behavioural Profile (associations/memberships/purchase habits)	
4. Customer Profile Give this target market a one- or two-word label, and then link the four profile descriptions into a single statement.	

Plan Write-Up: Weave your answers together into a paragraph, using bullet points when necessary.

C. GROWTH STRATEGY

Growth Strategy: What is your growth strategy (for example, acquisition, merger, new markets, new products)?

Current Market: How will you increase your current market's usage of your product or service on a per-customer basis?

New Applications: What new applications might there be for your product or service that would appeal to new markets?

New Markets: What new markets will you target in the future?

New Products: What new products could you upsell to your current customers in the future?

Plan Write-Up: Weave your answers together into a paragraph, using bullet points when necessary.

To build a sustainable business, you need a defined, sizable market. No matter how original your idea is, don't expect to operate in a competition-free environment. It's rare that you will enter any market without some sort of competition, even if it comes from the customer himself (think of a lawn-cutting service that competes with a homeowner who likes cutting his or her own lawn). In the next chapter, you'll look at the competitive landscape of your industry, and how you plan to compete to win customers.

CHAPTER 14

WHO IS YOUR COMPETITION?

"This is acceleration capital for you to perhaps achieve your goals, which is staying ahead of five other guys that are doing this."
—Dragon to Pitcher

SECTION 4: COMPETITIVE ANALYSIS

Describe your direct and indirect competitors. Identify their weaknesses. Position your business model against their weaknesses.

You don't need to be the first to market to build a sustainable business. The chocolate bar wasn't invented by Milton Hershey, the Mars family, or the Cadbury family. It was invented by the Fry family in England back in 1847. Facebook didn't introduce us to the concept of social networking—social networking had already been made popular by Friendster and MySpace. Apple and Microsoft weren't the first to show us what a graphical user interface was—that was Xerox. And Henry Ford didn't invent the automobile—he came up with a concept for mass production. History shows that you don't have to be the first mover in a market space to capitalize on it. You just need a business model, a competitive advantage, and a go-to-market strategy to win enough customers over your competition to meet your company's vision, mission, and goals.

In fact, competition can be a good thing. The overriding benefit of having competition is that you won't have to spend an enormous amount of money teaching people why your product or service is needed. Instead, you can spend your resources educating a segment of the public about why your product or service is original and/or better than the competition.

One way to do that is to enter a mature market with a green version of a business that already exists. The team from Evergreen Memories, visitors to the Dragons' Den, compete in the corporate and party-favours market that is already heavily saturated with competition from mugs, logos, key rings, and other disposable tchotchkes that many people soon throw away. So they came up with a green product that won't end up in landfills and will last for years to come. Pitcher Margot Woodworth showed the Dragons one product, but she has multiple SKUs based on her greenhouse business.

EVERGREEN MEMORIES

Pitcher: Margot Woodworth, Season 5, Episode 19

Focus: Finding Your Competitive Advantage

"I'm going to show you today that money does grow on trees . . . I'm sure all of you have been to a wedding or a big corporate event at one time, and you've received [gift] items [that you end up throwing away]. Evergreen Memories has come up with an eco-friendly solution so we do not fill the landfills. These tree seedlings are packaged in a 100% bio-degradable plastic bag and the [logoed] tags are printed on 100% recycled paper. In the [bags] are seeds, so after the event you can plant your tree and you can also plant your tag."

—Pitcher to Dragons

PRODUCT DESCRIPTION

Eco-friendly gifts, including tree seedlings, that can be given away at weddings and corporate events.

DRAGONS' DEN BY THE NUMBERS

- **The Ask:** $73,000 for 20% of the business
- **Company Valuation:** $365,000
- **The Deal:** $70,000 for 30% of the business
- **$200,000:** Sales in the first six months this year
- **3–4:** The number of weeks that the tree seedlings will last without water
- **100%:** Biodegradability percentage of the plastic wrap they use
- **15,000:** The number of tree seedlings they sold to Honda last year

Pitcher Margot Woodworth shows the Dragons her living-memory seedling.

SECTION 4: COMPETITIVE ANALYSIS

The competitive analysis section of your business plan describes the alternative solutions in the marketplace and how you plan to position your product or service against them. The purpose of a competitive analysis is to communicate an understanding of your competition, and how you plan to capitalize on their weaknesses. This section of your business plan should discuss and defend your competitive advantage by describing the following:

A. **Competition:** The basis for competition in your industry, such as the cost, feature, or service component that most businesses in your category compete on. For example, *grocery stores compete on price and service.* It's important to include your direct and indirect competitors, their strengths, and their weaknesses. This includes any alternatives that customers can use to solve the problem that your product or service addresses. For example, *Coke and Pepsi are direct competitors, while Coke and coffee are indirect competitors.*

B. **Competitive Advantage:** How your product or service offering has a sustainable edge in the marketplace.

C. Barriers to Entry: Hurdles that new competitors would have to overcome to enter the market. This includes any legal, regulatory, or market-entry hurdles that your competitors will face. For example, *a patented process can keep competitors at bay for a few years until they figure out a way to work around your patent.*

A. Competition
Basis for Competition

It's important to understand the basis for competition in your industry so that you can compete effectively. Once you have this knowledge, you can decide on a "me too" strategy and compete head to head, or you can pick a strategy that changes the nature of the game. The overriding basis for competition in most markets could be any one of the following:

- **Price:** The competition for customers based primarily on the price of your product or service.
- **Quality:** The competition for customers based on the grade of your product or service. The quality of a product or service is measured by its ability to deliver on its promises and satisfy customers.
- **Distribution:** The competition for customers based on your ability to secure distribution or shelf space for your product or service.
- **Scale:** The competition for customers based on your access to resources necessary to produce your product. Scale is the ability to grow your business to a volume high enough to absorb significant upfront capital costs.
- **Other Bases of Competition:** The competition for customers may also be based on the performance, convenience, speed, feature innovation, support service, design, or even packaging of your product or service.

Direct vs. Indirect Competition

Competition is not always what it seems. You can have direct competition, which has a product or service that is similar to yours. Or you can have indirect competition, which addresses the same customer need that your product does, but in a different way. So, a tax-preparation service competes with tax software. A restaurant competes with home cooking. Public transportation competes with the automobile. And the six o'clock news competes with online news. Though you may not have a competitor who does exactly what you do, you still have competition. Something or someone is always competing for the minds and dollars of your customers. A competitor can be anything that your ideal customer sees as an alternative way to address their needs. Be aware of who you are competing with so that anyone who reads your business plan knows that you understand your business environment and how to maintain your own edge in the market. In this section of your business plan, describe who your competitors are, and their competitive advantage in the marketplace.

B. Competitive Advantage

Once you have thoroughly analyzed and brainstormed every conceivable source of competition to your product or service, and the overriding basis for competition in each of your chosen markets, identify your own sustainable edge in the marketplace by looking at the following elements:

- **Cost Advantage:** Do you have an operating process that enables you to charge the lowest price in the marketplace?
- **Feature:** Do you have a selling feature or characteristic (for example, attribute, name awareness, packaging, etc.) that makes your product or service superior?
- **Support Service:** Is there a characteristic of your support service (for example, usage assistance, guarantees, warranties, phone support, credit terms, etc.) that gives you a sustainable advantage in the marketplace?

C. Barriers to Entry

A business concept that can be readily copied, or a market that is easy to enter, is not the most attractive investment. An investor's return on investment is driven by profit and exit value, and if that profit is high initially, an investor knows that you will attract competition. If there are few obstacles for someone else to overcome in order to set up shop, your business becomes less attractive as an investment opportunity. The types of hurdles you should discuss in this section of your business plan include the following:

- **Legal Barriers:** Do you currently have a patent or other proprietary asset that would prevent a new competitor from readily copying your product or service?

- **Regulatory Barriers:** Are there a number of costly or time-consuming regulatory requirements for entering your industry?
- **Capital Cost:** Does your type of business require a significant investment to enter the market space?
- **Technological Barriers:** Do you have a process that is hard to replicate due to cost or innovation?

DRAGON LORE

Competitive analysis is not a one-and-done exercise. New competitors are always lurking around the corner, and will enter your market as soon as they smell profit. Competitive analysis is something you should do on an ongoing basis.

No market is more competitive than the payment-processing industry. But if you are able to do something disruptive, then you can crack just about any market, no matter how entrenched the market leaders are. The team from UseMyBank Services (now known as UseMyServices) used a go-to-market strategy to tap into a growing fear of disclosing personal credit card information when shopping online. They are so confident in their solution that they turned down one of the biggest offers ever made in the Dragons' Den—$1 million from all five Dragons together.

USEMYBANK SERVICES

Pitcher: Joseph Iuso and Brian Crozier, Season 4, Episode 18

BUSINESS MODEL

A payment-processing service that earns a profit of approximately 50% on payment-processing fees.

PROBLEM

Some people are reluctant to use their credit cards when shopping online, because they fear that websites may be insecure and their personal information may be stolen.

SOLUTION

An online payment solution that allows you to pay for your online purchases from your own bank account while keeping your personal information confidential. UseMyBank Services is presented as another payment option at the point of checkout. The software goes to your bank, confirms the funds, and in real time tells the online retailer that the purchase is confirmed.

GO-TO-MARKET

UseMyBank Services has 45 banks signed up, and is used in nine countries.

TEAM

Brian Crozier has worked in marketing and credit card processing. Joseph Iuso has worked in self-service banking for the past 20 years.

FINANCIALS

The Ask: $1,000,000 for 5% equity in the company
Company Valuation: $20,000,000
Revenues: $5,000,000 in fees already
The Deal: $0 (the pitchers turned down an offer from all five Dragons of $1,000,000 for 40% of the company)

Pitcher Joseph Iuso demonstrating his online payment-processing service.

SELF-STUDY WORKSHOP: Competitive Analysis

For this section of your business plan, draft your talking points first by answering the relevant questions below. Then weave your answers together into a paragraph or two, using bullet points when necessary, and tables or diagrams if appropriate for each of A, B, and C.

COMPETITIVE ANALYSIS

A. Competition
B. Competitive Advantage
C. Barriers to Entry

A. COMPETITION

Basis for Competition: What is the basis for competition in your industry? (For example, product design, cost, service, etc.)

Direct Competition: Who are your three to five direct competitors? These are businesses that sell similar solutions to your type of product or service. (Don't limit your description to businesses within your geographic region.) What are their relevant strengths and weaknesses?

Indirect Competition: Who are your three to five indirect competitors? These are the companies that sell products or services that are different than yours, but that solve the same problem. For example, tax preparation software vs. a tax preparation service, or tea vs. coffee. (Don't limit your description to businesses within your geographic region.) What are their relevant strengths and weaknesses?

Plan Write-Up: Weave your answers together into a paragraph, using bullet points to break down dense information. Add a competitive matrix using the chart samples below.

DIRECT COMPETITORS

Competitor	Strengths	Weaknesses

INDIRECT COMPETITORS

Competitor	Strengths	Weaknesses

B. COMPETITIVE ADVANTAGE

Competitive Advantage: What is your competitive advantage, and why is it sustainable? Do you have a cost, feature, or service advantage over your competitors?

Plan Write-Up: Summarize your competitive advantage in one or two sentences.

C. BARRIERS TO ENTRY

Barriers to Entry: What barriers to entry make it difficult for new competitors to enter your market? (For example, start-up costs, regulatory barriers such as time-consuming or expensive licensing requirements, intellectual-property acquisition costs, etc.)

Plan Write-Up: Weave your answers together into a paragraph, using bullet points when necessary.

Business is a competition, and you have to compete to win in whatever market you choose to operate. If you want to be around long enough to profit from your business, create a business model that's built on a sustainable competitive advantage in your market. In the next chapter, you'll create a succinct description of how you plan to make money.

Chapter 15

How Do You Plan to Make Money?

"You don't need any more money—you just need to get orders."
  —Dragon to Pitcher

SECTION 5: BUSINESS MODEL

Create a list of your potential revenue streams. Define the product, customer, and pricing method for each revenue stream on your list. Create a declarative statement of how you plan to make money.

Nothing in this world is truly free, but "free" can certainly be a great business strategy. In the technology sector, businesses use free-pricing models to make money all the time. Mozilla Firefox, the big player in the free Web browser market, has been paid millions in the past to make Google their default search engine. Square Inc. will send almost anyone a free credit card-processing machine that plugs into an Android device, iPhone, or iPad, with very few questions asked. Then the company charges a 2.75% fee for every transaction made using their device. And mobile apps are often free, but then charge a fee for some added service. For example, a music app will identify radio songs for free, and then offer to sell us the songs that we hear.

But free-pricing models are not limited to the high-tech sector. Local community papers give away the news for free, knowing that their readership will help them sell advertising. Mary Kay independent sales reps give away free facials, knowing that you'll then need to buy their cosmetics if you want to repeat the process. And, of course, many financial and insurance firms give advice for free, and then charge us a commission on the mutual funds and insurance products that they have recommended that we buy (or they could receive a trail fee of X% per year on the fund as long as you stay in the fund).

In each of these examples, "free" is not a sales promotion like a food sample you get at the grocery store, or a promotional product at a corporate event. These businesses have a real strategy for making money—sometimes unbeknownst to the customer. The point is, a business model should be flexible in the beginning until you find a market that can help turn your product or service into a revenue-generating asset. Start with obvious revenue sources like the end-user. Then brainstorm alternative ways to get people to pay you. Just do everything you possibly can to find the most profitable way to generate revenue. And do it fast, because markets shift, and someone somewhere probably has the same idea you do. When two young preteen entrepreneurs, Caleb and Lars Krohn, showed up to the Dragons' Den, they had bags of entrepreneurial spirit and were bubbling with ideas about how to reach their customers. And they ended up having one of the show's favourite pitches of all time.

LIQUID HOT CHOCOLATE

Pitchers: Caleb Krohn and Lars Krohn, Season 6, Episode 11

Focus: Create a Flexible Business Model

"All hot chocolate mixes are powders that clump in water and hardly dissolve . . . Here's what we're going to do. Liquid hot chocolate in a portion pack. No mess. No fuss. No dust. First we're going to think outside the package. Then we're going to push the envelope. Then we'll take it to the next level. Hit the ground running. Think big. Start small. Raise the bar. Last but not least we're gonna put a stick in the package . . . We're going to package hot chocolate in a different way . . . the opposite of how it's been packaged. It's new. We think this product would be ideal on the kids' menu at any franchise restaurant, or it could be private labelled for any existing hot chocolate manufacturer, or we could just retail it ourselves. We're in talks with a local sales rep for an international cereal company, and we have a local distributor that's agreed to promote and sell our product."

—Pitcher to Dragons

PRODUCT DESCRIPTION

Liquid hot chocolate in a portion pack.

DRAGONS' DEN BY THE NUMBERS

- **The Ask:** $50,000 for 75% equity
- **Company Valuation:** $66,667
- **The Deal:** $50,000 for 75% equity
- **7:** The number of seconds it took the pitchers to agree to a deal
- **5:** The number of go-to-market strategies considered by the pitchers

Caleb Krohn and Lars Krohn pitching Liquid Hot Chocolate to the Dragons.

SECTION 5: BUSINESS MODEL

The single most important factor in the long-term success of a business is a business model. A business model is a strategy for making money. The purpose of a business model is to convert a product or service into an asset that generates repeat revenue. The business model section of your business plan should evolve over time as you learn more about your customers. Ideally, it will include the following sections:

A. **Value Chain:** Describe the links in the value chain that your product will pass through from you to the customer. This could include franchisees, independent sales reps, wholesalers, and retail outlets.

B. **Product/Market Fit:** State what you sell, and who you sell it to.

C. **Revenue Model:** Describe who's paying you, how much they are paying, and the logic behind how you charge for your product or service.

D. **Scalability:** Describe how you plan to grow your business while reducing costs over time.

A. Value Chain

If you want to convert your product or service into a revenue-generating asset, it's important to understand the traditional value chain in your industry. A value chain refers to a series of entities through which your product or service passes before it reaches the customer. Each entity adds value to your product or service along the way. In many cases, the entrepreneur handles the entire value chain, from research and development, to packaging, to delivery. But that's not always the most effective route. Your business model might be to occupy one or more links of the value chain by adding value to someone else's product or service. Or you could just come up with an idea and license it to someone else. To illustrate how a value chain works, consider a cosmetics product, and how value is added at each stage of the go-to-market process:

- **Research and Development (R&D):** Comes up with the product.
- **Manufacturing:** Builds the product.
- **Packaging:** Packages the product so that it protects the product and appeals to the customer.
- **Logistics:** Transports the product from point A to point B.
- **Marketing:** Establishes distribution agreements and generates customer demand.
- **Retail:** Makes the product available to the consumer and provides live product demonstrations.

In this section of your business model, describe what the value chain is, where you fit in it, and your role in adding value to it.

B. Product/Market Fit

Until you find a customer for your product or service, you are really an inventor. And an invention without a paying customer is not a business. For many inventors finding a market for their product (or service) is not always obvious. For example, if you invent a new type of pen that doesn't need ink, you might find it incredibly difficult to convince retailers to stock your product if you don't have actual sales. However, if you reposition your product as a promotional product, you might find it much easier to generate sales. In this section of your business model description, describe your product/market fit. Specifically, describe who your product is for and why they will buy it from you. For example, we sell inkless pens to business owners who use them as promotional products.

C. Revenue Model

When a business plan fails, it's because of a weak or poorly chosen business model. The core of every business plan should be a well-thought-out and proven business model. At the heart of that business model is how you make money (a.k.a. a revenue model). The most popular business models currently include one or a combination of the following model types:

- **Producer Business Model:** You produce and sell your own product or service directly or through intermediaries.
- **Merchant Business Model:** You set up an online or brick-and-mortar store and sell the products of others.
- **Agency Business Model:** You set up shop to bring buyers and sellers together, taking a fee for each transaction.
- **Franchising Business Model:** You hone your business model and then allow other entrepreneurs to license it for a fee.
- **Licensing Business Model:** You hone your product or service and then license it to a product manufacturer or a service provider.

D. Scalability

The Dragons always talk about scaling your business. What they mean is, will you be able to grow your business and will you have the production capacity in place to handle large volumes of customers? For example, if you were the inventor of the Banana Guard from Season 4,

Episode 15, would you be able to handle a sudden order for 22,000 units? In this section of your business model, you need to discuss the systems you have in place that will enable your business to generate and support higher and higher unit volumes, without stressing your financial and human resources. Most investors will not be interested in a business unless it is scalable because returns come from profit growth, and profit growth typically comes from revenue growth.

Business Model Summary

You can have multiple business models in the same business. Be aware, though, that having too many business models will leave your business unfocused and your customers confused. Just to recap, for each business model in your business, describe the following:

- **Product (or Service) Sold:** The tangible item (or intangible service) that people are willing to pay you for. For example, reusable plastic containers for storing, organizing, and transporting empty beer, wine, and liquor bottles.
- **Customers Served:** The type of customer who will value your product or service the most. In the above example, this would be the customers who purchase alcohol.
- **Repeat Revenue Model:** The method of charging for your product or service that will sustain your business, such as renting, selling at a per-unit price, or licensing your invention to a manufacturer in exchange for a royalty fee. You could charge $10 retail and $8 wholesale per box, for example.

DRAGON LORE

There may be more than one way to earn money from your product or service. Look for creative revenue streams that either build on, or diverge from, traditional models.

Every business model should be considered a work in progress until you have demonstrated proof of concept. What starts out as a clear path to profitability on paper can change rapidly when the market rejects your idea. When the team from Smart Casing approached the Dragons, they were clear enough on their vision for their product to get two competing offers from the Dragons—even though they only had two orders at the time.

SMART CASING

Pitchers: Pranav Sood and Xi Yan, Season 6, Episode 20

BUSINESS MODEL

The company charges $30 to $40 per phone to put corporate logos and colours on the hard casings of corporate-issued phones—with 70% to 80% profit margins per phone.

PROBLEM

Companies providing phones to their employees are missing out on a branding opportunity.

SOLUTION

A custom design created with the company, followed by a five-minute installation process that customizes a corporate-issued smartphone with company colours and screen-printed logos.

GO-TO-MARKET

The pitchers plan to prove the concept using a direct-sales model to sell to companies that provide work phones to their employees. They then want to use proof of concept to establish strategic relationships with cellphone carriers who can offer the service to their corporate clients. The pitchers also have a direct-to-consumer sales model for individuals who want to decorate their phones.

TEAM

Pranav Sood is a recent business school graduate with some experience in a start-up telecom company, and Xi Yan is one of the technicians who actually does the installation work on the phones.

FINANCIALS

The Ask: $50,000 for 20% equity in the company
Company Valuation: $250,000
Current-Year Revenue Projection: After three months in business, they have two orders, one for 10 units and one for 50 units
The Deal: $50,000 for 40% of the business

Xi Yan from Smart Casings applying a corporate logo and colours to a phone on *Dragons' Den*.

SELF-STUDY WORKSHOP: Business Model

For this section of your business plan, draft your talking points first by answering the relevant questions below. Then weave your answers together into a paragraph or two, using bullet points when necessary, and tables or diagrams if appropriate for each of A, B, C, and D.

BUSINESS MODEL

A. Value Chain
B. Product/Market Fit
C. Revenue Model
D. Scalability

A. VALUE CHAIN

Identify the two to three key players in your industry. Describe the traditional links in the value chain of your product or service category. Be specific about who adds value and how. Discuss how your value chain is similar to or different from the traditional model.

Two to Three Key Players: Who are the major players in your industry?
R&D: Who conceives of and designs the product that the major players sell?
Production: How is your product or service produced?

Distribution: Who establishes the relationships with the outlets that make the product or service physically available to the ultimate consumer? For example, are there distributors or agents who can market your product to retailers on your behalf?

Logistics: Who transports the product to the outlet that sells it?

Sales Outlets: Who makes the product or service physically available to the ultimate consumer?

Plan Write-Up: *Weave your answers together into a paragraph to summarize the traditional value chain in your industry, and explain how your business is positioned in it or against it.*

B. PRODUCT/MARKET FIT

Customers Served: Make a list of every potential customer who could pay you for your product or service. Explain why they would pay you, and describe how you would get paid.

Product or Service Sold: For each revenue stream and customer served, name the product or service that could be sold to that person, business entity, or organization.

Plan Write-Up: *Weave your answers together into a paragraph to summarize your product/market fit.*

C. REVENUE MODEL

What is your revenue model? Why did you choose it? Why will it be effective? If you have a different revenue model for each product you sell or customer you serve, mention that in this section. Your model might be one of the standard models listed in the Revenue Model section above (for example, producer model, merchant model, etc.), or it could be something else that doesn't fit into one of these categories.

Plan Write-Up: *In one to two paragraphs, summarize your revenue model and your core revenue streams.*

D. SCALABILITY

Why is your business model scalable? Specifically, how is your business set up to handle varying levels of sales volume?

Plan Write-up: *In one or two paragraphs, summarize why your business is scalable.*

A product or service is not a business without a profitable and repeat-revenue model, and customers who are willing to pay your price. Once you have established a business model, the next step is to market and sell your products or services. In the next chapter, you'll create an achievable go-to-market strategy that includes channels, strategic partners, a marketing program, and a way to get commitments from customers.

CHAPTER 16

HOW WILL YOU GET CUSTOMERS?

"You only get one chance to make an elephant type of sale."
—Dragon to Pitcher

SECTION 6: SALES AND MARKETING STRATEGY

State your product/market focus. Describe what will be your most effective sales channels, and how you plan to establish them. Create an efficient marketing campaign to draw customers to the channel. Leverage strategic relationships where possible to achieve rapid market penetration.

"Find a need and fill it." Many entrepreneurs take heed of this deceptively simple premise when they first launch their businesses. They come up with a unique product or service feature, and they focus their sales and marketing efforts around that feature and label it a unique selling proposition (USP). Then, for one reason or another, they stop paying attention to their copycat or more innovative competitors, and what was once unique soon becomes a standard selling proposition that every customer expects.

Polaroid started out as the only camera to offer instant photographs, and today every digital camera in the world provides us with instant images that can be printed out on a printer. The BlackBerry began its life as the only phone that could support email, and today it's being buried by what Lars Bodenheimer calls the "smartphone avalanche." And at one time Quiznos was the only submarine-sandwich chain that toasted its subs, but now almost every other sandwich chain does it too. Each of these companies eventually ran into troubled waters because their original ideas ended up being copied or out-innovated by their competition.

The problem with many companies is that the entrepreneurial mindset that helps launch great products and services gets lost behind a managerial mindset that focuses on executing an established plan. When managers should be constantly rebooting their businesses with innovations—ideas like cameras and phones that charge themselves wirelessly; shopping carts that give running totals of purchases; or cars that can be maintained with easy-to-replace parts—they settle for managing the products and markets they already have. And this type of path never ends well. Polaroid is struggling to adapt its product to a digital world; the BlackBerry is no longer ranked among the top five smartphones on the market; and Quiznos is rebuilding its outlet volume after shutting down many of its locations. If you want to grow your business, start with a unique selling proposition that currently sticks. Then change it over time as the market and your competition evolve. Never lose the entrepreneurial spirit that got you into business in the first place.

Pitcher Nancy Yowney came into the Dragons' Den with a business that she had been running on the side while working her day job in a fitness centre. She created a simple magnet that is inserted into the stem of a boutonnière or a corsage so that you don't have to use a stick pin, and she sells her product to florists across the country. Free publicity from being featured on the television show *The Bachelorette* helped secure a deal with a U.S. wholesaler that services 50,000 flower shops across the country. One Dragon made a deal to help her build the inventory she needs to reach these new customers.

BOUTBUDDY

Pitcher: Nancy Yowney, Season 6, Episode 16

Focus: Find a business model for your product.

"With the Dragons' help and connections, I can go worldwide a lot sooner—there are 1 million boutonnières made every day."
—Pitcher to Dragons

PRODUCT DESCRIPTION

A magnet that attaches a boutonnière or corsage to clothing.

DRAGONS' DEN BY THE NUMBERS

- **The Ask:** $50,000 for 10% of the business
- **Company Valuation:** $500,000
- **The Deal:** $50,000 for 25% of the business
- **$150,000:** The amount of revenue over four years (while Yowney worked part-time)
- **300,000:** The number of Boutbuddies sold in Canada to date
- **50,000:** The number of flower shops serviced by the largest wholesaler in the United States

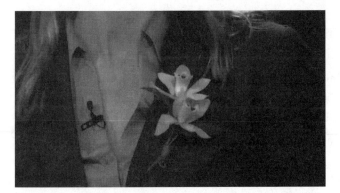

Pitcher Nancy Yowney with her Boutbuddy, featured on *The Bachelorette*.

SECTION 6: SALES AND MARKETING STRATEGY

In this section of your business plan, provide a succinct description of your sales and marketing strategy. This is not a detailed marketing plan, just the highlights. A full 10- to 25-page marketing plan should be written separately at another time, whereas an investor-ready business plan should be 10 to 40 pages in total. This section should be succinct and to the point.

A sales and marketing strategy describes where you plan to make your product or service available to customers, and how you plan to attract customers to those channels. The purpose of a sales and marketing strategy is to attract and win customers. This section of your business plan should include the following topics:

A. **Positioning:** Your product/market fit, and how you are uniquely positioned to capture that niche.

B. **Pricing Strategy:** How you calculate and justify your price level.

C. **Sales Strategy:** Direct sales vs. indirect sales.

D. **Marketing Strategy:** How you will get the word out, including advertising, public relations, and publicity.

E. **Strategic Relationships:** Agreements with other businesses or entities that help you go to market faster.

F. **Sales Forecast:** The sales volume you expect to achieve.

A. Positioning

At the heart of your sales and marketing strategy is a unique selling proposition, or USP. A USP is the feature, attribute, or benefit of your product or service that *currently* makes it unique in your market. Since great strategies ultimately get copied, your USP will need to evolve over time—what starts out as your signature today will become a common feature that all of your competitors will offer tomorrow. In this section of your plan, describe your USP, and why it is defensible, based on any of the following criteria:

• a problem that only your product or service solves
• a unique feature of your product or service
• a unique benefit of your product or service
• a unique process of your product or service
• some other proprietary attribute or unique characteristic of your product or service

Keep your USP current by continuing to innovate, shopping your competition, and responding to new market entrants with product or service improvements. Also support your positioning with additional, or secondary, benefits that people will receive when they use your product or service.

B. Pricing Strategy

To figure out how much to charge, start with the money trail in your industry (i.e., who gets paid to do what). You're in business to provide a product or service that people are willing to pay you for. If you don't charge enough, you won't be in business long enough to keep your customers satisfied. The price you charge must cover your fixed and variable costs, your expenses, and the profit that's required to keep your business open, while at the same time being palatable to your customer base. You're not doing anyone any good if you have to shut your business down within five years because you can't afford to stay open.

You can establish a pricing strategy by creating a price floor and price ceiling, and a final price point that fits within that window. Make sure that it is low enough to generate the sales volume required to meet your sales forecast and business objectives. Be prepared to discuss the following:

- **Price Floor**: The absolute lowest price you could charge before you start losing money.
- **Price Ceiling:** The absolute highest price you could charge before you start losing your "ideal" customers.
- **Price Point:** The price level you end up charging.

Pricing Objectives and Strategy

Be prepared to justify your pricing strategy and price point to investors. If you plan to initially charge a high price to early adopters, so that you can build capital to fund future innovations, this is called a *skimming strategy*. If your goal is to penetrate the market rapidly with a disruptive innovation and a low price, this is called a *penetration-pricing strategy*. If your pricing objective is to match competition, so that non-price differences between the products or services can clearly stand out, this is called a *competitor-matching strategy*. And if your price levels are in place to reflect a specific level of quality in your product or service, then explain why your product or service will meet that standard. Readers of your business plan will need a rationale for every decision you make, so in this section, describe the rationale behind your pricing. Understanding why your prices are what they are gives stakeholders some insight into the long-term value of your price points.

Sales and Marketing Strategy

A sales and marketing strategy must incorporate marketing communications efforts that *pull* customers to your point of sale, and sales channels that *push* your products or services out to customers. Don't confuse the term "push" with being "pushy." To illustrate the difference, imagine picking up a newspaper and seeing an ad for a free wine-tasting event at a beautiful winery. The offer is compelling enough to "pull" you to the location. After you complete the free wine tasting and are enjoying the beautiful view, the sommelier pushes a bottle or two of your favourite wine on you. You put down your payment card and leave with a bottle of wine and a great experience, and everyone is happy. But if the sommelier becomes pushy, and tries selling you a whole case, then you probably won't come back.

In this section of your business plan, explain how you will use a combination of *marketing pull* and *sales push* to convert targeted prospects into paying customers. Start by defining your sales and marketing objectives:

- **Sales Objectives:** Sales objectives are typically quantifiable, such as X number of customers, $X of sales volume per year, or X% of market share by a certain date.
- **Marketing Objectives:** Marketing objectives can also be quantifiable in terms of frequency and reach, such as X% customer-satisfaction levels, or non-quantifiable, like education, awareness, or image building.

C. Sales Strategy

Very few new businesses have enough capital to launch a full-scale marketing campaign intended to pull the customer to the point of sale. Advertising, promotion, and publicity make up a trial-and-error process that can consume valuable resources, often with untrackable results. For many start-ups, the most cost-effective and efficient way to launch a business is to push products and services out to customers through direct and indirect sales channels that already have access to the customers. When you do this systematically, by launching one sales channel at a time, this is called "roll-out" strategy.

In this section of your business plan, describe your sales strategy, whether it's a direct or indirect strategy, and why it is the most effective path to the customer.

Direct Sales Channels

Unless you have been able to secure a distribution agreement, or have a healthy budget for hiring outside sales reps, the shortest distance between you and your customer may be a straight line. In business, that straight line is direct sales. No intermediaries, no retailer agreements, no razor-thin profit margins—just you pushing your products or services out to the customer. L.L. Bean started with a direct-sales campaign using a mailing list and a flyer.[1] Today it has over a billion dollars in revenue from using a version of the same direct-sales model that worked when it opened 100 years ago. Amazon.com started selling books directly over the Internet from a garage. Today it is a profitable company, has fulfillment centres around the world, and continues to sell inventory directly to its customers. It also helps over a million third-party direct sellers launch their own sales efforts using Amazon's marketplace and technology. And Dell Inc. started out by selling computers direct from a dorm room, and today it continues to sell the majority of its computers and products directly through its website and via a toll-free phone number. While not always the most financially efficient path to a customer, direct sales can be the fastest way to prove your concept so that you have more leverage when you approach indirect channels. Direct sales channels include the following:

DIRECT SALES CHANNELS*

Teleselling	Door to Door	Home Party Plans	Sales Calls	Direct Mail	Website
Use a phone list that you rent, buy, or build to call people who have previously shown an interest in your products or services.	Research neighbourhoods that meet your target-market profile and conduct door-to-door sales if it is legal in the area.	Find hosts who agree to hold in-home party events where you can demonstrate and sell your product or service to their guests.	Conduct in-person sales meetings with businesses, distributors, and individuals.	Rent, buy, or build a mailing list and then send out a mailer. Showcase your product and include a method for making a purchase.	Set up an e-commerce website and sell your products directly online.

* These are not hard and fast rules. Terminology and practices vary by industry.

Indirect Sales Channels

The other strategy for selling is to establish relationships with intermediaries who already have a relationship with the customer you are targeting. Not all products or services can be pushed through direct channels, because people *expect* to buy them through more established indirect channels. For example, we might buy strawberries at the side of the highway, or electronics over the Internet. But most of us wouldn't respond well to doctors making sales calls to talk about their services. We usually don't buy expensive watches from "sales reps" on the streets of Toronto. And we rarely buy prepared meals from people who make them in their garages. In many cases, indirect channels can even increase the perceived value of the product or service that you are selling. Getting into indirect sales channels requires sales calls, attendance at industry trade shows, marketing materials to back up sales calls, and, in many cases, visits to retail outlets. The costs involved vary by channel, with face-to-face meetings being the most expensive, and phone calls being the least expensive.

INDIRECT SALES CHANNELS*

Agent	Wholesaler	Distributor	Independent Stores	Regional Stores	National Stores
A third party who sells your product for a commission.	A third party who sells your product in bulk to distributors and retailers.	A third party who sells and distributes your product to retailers. In some cases, you might use resellers or value-added resellers (VARs).	Owner-operated stores. It is usually easier to get shelf space in these. In some cases you can sell on consignment.	Chain stores that operate in one geographic region of the country.	Chain stores that are located across multiple provinces or states. It is difficult to obtain shelf space in these.

* These are not hard and fast rules. Terminology and practices vary by industry.

D. Marketing Strategy

Most start-ups don't have the funding required to engage in full-scale awareness-building campaigns. Advertising is expensive, it requires trial-and-error testing, and the results are often untrackable. But marketing doesn't have to be expensive, and low-cost publicity, well-thought-out promotions, and trade show attendance (with or without a booth), can often lead to important introductions, strategic alliances, and, in some cases, broad market exposure. In this section of your business plan, explain how you plan to draw attention to your brand, and how your marketing efforts will support your sales channels.

MARKETING METHODS

Advertising	Promotion	Publicity	Trades Shows	Social Media
Paid media coverage, including newspaper, magazine, catalogue, TV, radio, direct-mail, or outdoor ads, or online advertising, including Google AdWords.	General awareness-building efforts, including workshops, websites, search engine optimization, giveaways, live demonstrations, and free-product giveaways to people who have influence over large numbers of potential customers.	Free media coverage for awards, breakthrough innovations, strategic alliances, or product news, through editors and media contacts who can be a third-party endorsement for your business. Generated through press releases, speeches, articles of interest, media site visits, product or service reviews, media interviews, and publicity stunts.	Events where you can demonstrate your product or service in front of a specific target market. Trade shows include consumer shows, business-to-business events, and government events.	Tools like Facebook, LinkedIn, and Twitter that connect you with others who are interested in hearing what you have to say, and who often endorse your product or service with positive comments that others can read.

Budgeting

If you do launch a marketing campaign, it is important to establish reach, frequency, and budgeting objectives. Objectives shouldn't be a limiting factor. In other words, don't let a pre-set budget keep you from taking advantage of an ad hoc promotion that you hadn't planned for. But do use budgeting as a guide for your decision making going forward. In this section of your plan, discuss your budget, and the assumptions you made to write it.

- **Percentage of Sales:** Committing a disciplined amount of funds on advertising, such as 5% of projected revenue, or an industry average.
- **Competitor Matching:** Spending what your competitors appear to be spending by tracking what they do, and matching what they do.
- **Affordability:** Spending based on what you have left after other expense obligations have been met.

E. Strategic Relationships: Go to Market Faster

Strategic relationships can help you go to market faster than you can on your own. A strategic relationship is an agreement with another business or entity that already has an established relationship with your ideal customers. Or they might have a business process that can help you go to market at a lower cost. Many strategic relationships will require that you give up some per-unit profit, but what you give up in lower margins can be made up in increased sales volume if you're still making a per-unit profit. Strategic relationships only work if the interests of all participants are aligned. For example, selling your product at a loss just to get shelf space at a big-box retailer could put you out of business unless it is only for a short period of time. The following are examples of strategic relationships that you should consider for your business:

STRATEGIC RELATIONSHIPS*

Private Labelling	Co-branding	Licensing	Franchising	Joint Ventures	Bundling
Allow another company to put its name on the product you produce, package, and deliver. e.g., No Name brand products at Loblaws grocery stores.	Incorporate your product or service with another brand, and include both logos on your packaging. e.g., Tim Hortons and Coldstone Creamery	Allow another company to produce, package, and deliver your product in exchange for a licensing fee that they pay you. e.g., Trivial Pursuit originally licensed their game to Selchow and Righter	License your business model to entrepreneurs who pay you a set-up + royalty fee in exchange for the use of your operating model, brand name, ongoing support, and advertising. e.g., Harvey's restaurant chain	Set up a new, temporary business entity with another business in order to enter a new market or capitalize on a business opportunity. e.g., MillerCoors	Persuade the producer of a complementary product to include your product with theirs, as a value add. e.g., Including your dental floss with every toothbrush that another company sells.

*Always seek legal advice before you sign any strategic-partnership agreements.

F. Sales Forecast

Every industry has a standard revenue model, and your sales forecast should summarize yours in a simple chart. A sales forecast describes where your sales will come from in the next twelve months to three years. Start by listing your products or services in a spreadsheet. Then list the sales that you project for each of them. For a restaurant, this may be as simple as breakfast sales, lunch sales, and dinner sales. For a software company, this may be boxed software, downloads, and upgrades. For a recycling firm, this may be retainer fees from corporations who have garbage that needs to be recycled, and raw-material fees from companies who want to reuse the raw materials. Your sales forecast can be stated however you like.

You can base your sales forecast on product, technology, or service sold, markets targeted, or fees charged, depending on how your product or service is sold. There are two ways to create a sales forecast:

- **Bottom Up:** Forecast sales by territory or market segment.
- **Top Down:** Forecast sales by the percentage of the market. Estimate the total market size by studying industry research reports, then estimate the percentage of the market that you will capture.

DRAGON LORE

Sales and marketing go hand in hand. The job of marketing is to draw positive attention to your brand. The job of sales is to convert customer attention into paying customers.

One way to draw positive attention to your brand is to do something that is good for the community. And if you can help politicians look good in the process, you might just have a business on your hands. Guy Chaham of Green Gym visited the Dragons' Den with all of his ducks in a row. He had a socially responsible concept, with revenue, satisfied customers, and a compelling value proposition already in place.

GREEN GYM

Pitcher: Guy Chaham, Season 6, Episode 9

BUSINESS MODEL

The pitcher charges $20,000 to municipalities for a basic set-up of outdoor gym equipment, which he installs in outdoor parks.

PROBLEM

People want to exercise outdoors on the same type of equipment that they use at indoor gyms. However, outdoor spaces lack a place to plug in such equipment.

SOLUTION

Outdoor resistance-based gym equipment that is very similar to indoor gym equipment—from cardio to strength-training equipment—but doesn't require power to run.

GO-TO-MARKET

Green Gym sells to municipalities that buy the equipment for outdoor green spaces, senior homes, schools, campgrounds, and playgrounds.

TEAM

Guy Chaham plans to create a federal safety standard for outdoor equipment that the government backs.

FINANCIALS

The Ask: $200,000 for 10% equity in the company
Company Valuation: $2,000,000
Revenue: $1.1 million for the current year, and projections of $2.4 million for next year
The Deal: $200,000 for 17.5% equity plus 6% royalty until the capital is paid back

Pitcher Guy Chaham and his team demonstrate Green Gym.

SELF-STUDY WORKSHOP: Sales and Marketing Strategy

For this section of your business plan, draft your talking points first by answering the relevant questions below. Then weave your answers together into a paragraph or two, using bullet points when necessary, and tables or diagrams if appropriate for each of A, B, C, D, E, and F.

SALES AND MARKETING STRATEGY

A. Positioning
B. Pricing Strategy
C. Sales Strategy
D. Marketing Strategy
E. Strategic Relationships
F. Sales Forecast

OVERVIEW

Key to Success: What will be the key to your sales and marketing success? What primary channel will you use, and what market share will you capture?

Sales and Marketing Objectives: What are your sales objectives? What are your marketing objectives?

Plan Write-Up: Weave your answers together into a paragraph.

A. POSITIONING

Product or Service Category: What product or service category are you competing in?

USP: What is your unique selling proposition in the markets you will compete in? Specifically, what feature, process, problem-solving attribute, benefit, or other fact about your product or service is currently your main selling point?

Secondary Benefits: What secondary benefits of your product stand out the most?

Target Market: What target market group in particular will be most responsive to this positioning?

Plan Write-Up: Weave your answers together into a paragraph, using bullet points to break down dense information.

B. PRICING STRATEGY

For each of your product or service categories, discuss the following:

Pricing Objective: What is your overall pricing objective? Are you looking for short-term profit, to match competitor prices, to build market share, or to establish a perception of high quality? Do you have a low-price, high-volume strategy, or a high-price, low-volume strategy?

Price Calculations: How do you calculate your price(s) (i.e., cost-based, market-based, competition-based)? If you have several products, list them and describe the pricing methodology for each.

Discounts: Will you be offering any periodic discounts to consumers? If you are selling through intermediaries, what volume deals, bonus units, allowances, or co-op contributions will you be making?

Price Justification: How do you justify your prices, and how does your marketing strategy help you achieve your sales (or revenue) and marketing objectives?

Brand Image: How does your price level reflect your brand image? What is your price level compared to your competition?

Sensitivity: Discuss the sensitivity of your target market to pricing, and how you will track and respond to the price sensitivity of your customers.

Price Floor: What is the lowest price you could charge and still generate a profit?

Price Ceiling: What is the highest price you could charge and still have customers willing to pay you?

Price Point: What price point(s) will generate the highest number of customers?

Plan Write-Up: Weave your answers together into paragraphs, using bullet points to break down dense information.

C. SALES STRATEGY

Sales Strategy: What is the strategy you will use to sell your product? Direct sales (mail order/door to door/home party plans/etc.)? Indirect sales (agent/distributor/third-party retailer/etc.)? Describe your sales strategy in two to three sentences, and explain why it is the most effective way to sell your product or service. Discuss the sales channels (and specific stores/distributors/agents where applicable) that you already have in place, those you are planning for in the future, and how much each channel will contribute as a percentage of overall sales.

Sales Cycle: How long is the sales cycle? In other words, how long does it take, on average, from the time you first make contact with a prospective customer to the time the customer places an order?

Payment: How will your customers pay for your products or services? Are there any payment terms?

Sales Incentives: What type of sales incentives will you offer and why?

Discounts: What type of discount pricing will you offer and why?

Rollout Strategy: What is your roll-out strategy? Use the chart sample below to answer this question.

Sales Channel	Specific Outlets	Date

Plan Write-Up: Weave your answers together into paragraphs, using bullet points to break down dense information.

D. MARKETING STRATEGY

Marketing Strategy: In two to three sentences, describe your marketing communications strategy. What will be the most effective tool for building awareness of your brand? Will you be targeting businesses, intermediaries, or end-users?

Communications Budget: What is your communications budget as a percentage of projected revenue?

Communications Objectives: What are your communications objectives? (For example, mass reach or niche penetration.)

Media Outlets: What specific media outlets attract your target audience? (For example print, online, or social media.) Can you identify by name some publications that reach your customers?

Publicity Tools: What publicity tools will you use to attract customers?

Referrals: Who will refer business to you and why?

Trade Shows: What trade shows attract your target audience?

Marketing Methods: What are your marketing methods? Use the chart sample below to answer this question.

Marketing Tactic	Description	Budget

Plan Write-Up: Weave your answers together into paragraphs, using bullet points to break down dense information.

E. STRATEGIC RELATIONSHIPS

Strategic Relationships: What strategic relationships have you established or will you establish in the future?

Co-branding: What other product or service would you be willing to co-brand yours with?

Licensing: What type of manufacturer could license your product (or service model)?

Franchising: Do you have a business model that lends itself to franchising?

Joint Ventures: Are there any markets that you *cannot* enter without partnering with another business? If so, what specific businesses would you be willing to establish a joint venture with?

Bundling: What types of products or services complement yours? What types of products or services would bundle your product with theirs as part of their offering?

Planning Strategic Relationships: What are your plans for establishing strategic relationships? Use the chart sample below to answer this question.

Strategic Relationships	Description	Budget

Plan Write-Up: Weave your answers together into paragraphs, using bullet points to break down dense information.

F. SALES FORECAST

Choose a sales-forecasting method that best fits your product/market focus. Then build your sales forecast and include one or more of the tables below in your business plan.

Option A) Projected Sales by Revenue Source (i.e., Product/Service)

SALES PROJECTION BY PRODUCT TYPE

Product/Service	Year 1	Year 2	Year 3	Year 4	Year 5
1					
2					
3					
4					
Total Sales Projection					

Option B) Projected Sales by Market Segment

PROJECTED SALES BY MARKET SEGMENT

Market Segment	Year 1	Year 2	Year 3	Year 4	Year 5
1					
2					
3					
4					
Total Sales Projection					

Option C) Projected Sales by Fees Charged to Customers

PROJECTED SALES BY FEES CHARGED TO CUSTOMERS

Fees Charged	Year 1	Year 2	Year 3	Year 4	Year 5
1					
2					
3					
4					
Total Sales Projection					

Most start-ups have limited marketing budgets, and are often better served by finding channels through which to sell their products or services than spending valuable resources trying to "pull" customers in with trial-and-error marketing campaigns. But creativity and innovation are what makes the entrepreneur tick. Given all of the social media, publicity, and online marketing options available, a well-thought-out marketing campaign is within reach of just about everyone with a computer, some skills, and some time. However, you can't execute a plan without a team. In the next chapter, we'll talk about the people who will execute your business plan.

Part IV

Management Structure and Organization

Describe the team that you have in place to execute your business plan.

CHAPTER 17

WHO WILL EXECUTE YOUR PLAN?

"I'm comfortable that you are going to grow this thing. If it's not going to be [one company] licensing, someone else is going to grab it."
—Dragon to Pitcher

SECTION 7: MANAGEMENT AND ORGANIZATION

Set up a basic management team, even if it's only one person. Create an advisory board of key people who can act as mentors. Develop a hiring plan for critical staffing needs. Have outside professional advisers who you can turn to on short notice.

We've all seen our favourite retailers suddenly disappear. In Canada, Blockbuster shut down, and Radio Shack was bought out. In the United States, Borders bookstores went bankrupt and then closed for good. What's next? Hardware stores, office-supply stores, clothing shops? It's already happening. Why is this happening? Or, more importantly, how is this happening? One reason is that we, as consumers, walk into a store to touch and feel a product, then we go online and buy it for a cheaper price. We've all done it—or soon will. It's called *showrooming*, and we do it with electronics, books, home appliances, and any other product that can be easily shipped. We do it because it's cheaper to buy online, and because there are no apparent consequences. And we do it because the managers of these once-great businesses did nothing to stop us. Instead of engineering new business models to keep up with the times, they managed the business models they already had.

Businesses are meant to be run by people who think like entrepreneurs and execute like managers. The two mindsets are almost antithetical, but any successful venture requires both skill sets. The entrepreneur figures out a way to capitalize on new markets that are ripe for innovation, and how to respond to sudden market shifts, while the manager works flaw-lessly to execute the operating model that underlies the business that the entrepreneur came up with.

Investors know this simple truism, and that's why the team section of your business plan is such a critical component. The ideal team has domain expertise and deep market experi-ence in permanent roles, with cross-functional support for the more temporary roles such as marketing, communications, design, and annual tax preparation.

When Maggie Bill pitched her multi-purpose invention, The Maggie Dress, on *Dragons' Den*, her 20 years of experience in the industry were an integral part of convincing the Dragons that she could execute her business plan. She showed how creativity and deep mar-ket experience can help you crack even the toughest barriers to entry. Having been a fashion stylist, she was able to use her experience with celebrities to design and test a dress for people who don't have the perfect body shape or size.

THE MAGGIE DRESS

Pitchers: Maggie Bill & Judy Tyson, Season 4, Episode 13

FOCUS: YOUR IDEAL TEAM

> "The Maggie Dress is something that I invented about two and a half years ago . . . I've been a fashion stylist and buyer for about 20 years, and dressed women of all ages, sizes, and insecurities . . . And I feel that if this product is promoted on a global level, I feel that it will become really an inherent go-to staple in women's closets around the world. It's all one dress . . . Let me just show you what I can do with this dress."
> —Pitcher to Dragons

PRODUCT DESCRIPTION

A dress that can be stylized many ways to adapt to, and flatter, different body shapes.

DRAGONS' DEN BY THE NUMBERS

- **The Ask:** $75,000 for 20% of the business
- **Company Valuation:** $375,000

- **The Deal:** $100,000 for 25% of the business
- **$47,000:** The revenue that pitcher Maggie brought in after one day of selling her product on The Shopping Channel
- **$130:** The retail price of The Maggie Dress
- **9:** The number of models Maggie Bill brought with her to the Dragons' Den.

Pitcher Maggie Bill demonstrating her product, The Maggie Dress, on a model she brought to *Dragons' Den*.

SECTION 7: MANAGEMENT AND ORGANIZATION

The entrepreneurial graveyard is riddled with millions of great ideas that had no viable action plan. You can have the most wonderful idea in the world, but without the right team around you, you'll never get it off the ground. Teams get products and services to market faster than individuals can do it themselves, and investors know this. The following are key talking points to include in this section of your business plan:

Human Resources Strategy: The overall strategy for how your business will be staffed.

A. **Business Organization:** How your business is set up.

B. **Management Team:** Key personnel on your team who are responsible for operating important functions of the business.

C. **Advisory Board:** Paid or unpaid members of your team who agree to provide advice to you on an as-needed basis.

D. **Professional Support:** Paid consultants who provide arm's-length advice to you as needed about specific business, legal, or financial questions.

E. **Hiring Needs:** Task- or project-oriented personnel who staff your business on a daily basis.

Human Resources Strategy

In this section of your business plan, include a brief opening statement that describes the following elements of your team:

- **Culture:** The values that will define your company and what you expect of your staff.
- **Talent Pool:** Where you will find your staff.
- **Training Requirements:** What sort of training your staff will need. Can you hire non-skilled workers who can be trained? Or must you hire highly skilled workers who have previous experience?

A. Business Organization

Ownership

In this section of your business plan, describe who owns your business. If you are looking for a partner or outside investment, be sure to seek legal and accounting advice so that you fully understand what you are getting into. You could end up with a legal and administrative nightmare if you provide ownership equity to an investor or an employee who leaves before you have received enough in return to warrant the ownership position they have taken in the company.

One way that corporations protect themselves is by setting up employee stock ownership plans (ESOPs) that give employees the feeling of ownership in the business, but with strings attached. With ESOPs, employees earn stock over time, shares vest over time, and the shares are subject to forfeiture if the employee leaves early. If you do decide to explore this route, your ESOP must comply with government regulations, so be sure to seek appropriate legal advice before going down this road.

Location

Deciding where to locate your business can be a decision based on cost or proximity to suppliers, customers, or a specific talent pool. It can even be a lifestyle choice of the entrepreneur if location is not relevant. In this section, state the location of your business and when your business was or will be formed there.

Licenses and Permits

Every industry is different, and subject to different government regulations. It is important for you to research the federal and provincial regulations required to run your type of business. A good place to start your research is an industry association. In this section of your plan, briefly describe the licenses, permits, and insurance requirements that your business is subject to. Also state your progress to date in securing those licenses and permits.

Legal Form of Business

Once you have worked out your goals for your business, you should strongly consider meeting with a business attorney or chartered accountant who can make a solid recommendation about the legal form of the business. There are many issues to consider when choosing your business structure. These include:

- **Taxation:** How the business structure is taxed.
- **Administration:** How much work you will have to do to administer the entity.
- **Protection:** How protected your personal assets are from the liabilities of the business.

You will be more than compensated for the hundreds of dollars you spend seeking professional advice with fewer headaches down the road. There are several types of business structures to choose from, four of which are as follows:

LEGAL FORMS OF BUSINESS

Sole Proprietorship	Partnership	Corporation	Co-operative
A single-person entity, a.k.a. a business registration, where you are not legally separate from your business. All of your personal assets are at risk in the event of a lawsuit. It's very easy to set up and run, and income and losses flow through to your personal tax return. You can also sell your business relatively easily.	A multi-person entity where you and your general partners are not legally separate from the business. All of your personal assets (and your general partners' assets) are at risk in the event of a lawsuit. Variations include limited partnerships and limited liability partnerships for professionals, where some liability protection is available for certain partners.	A separate legal entity that allows multiple investors to have limited liability and a proportionate share of the profits. Can lead to double taxation since the entity itself is taxed and the shareholders are taxed on any distributions that are made by the entity. Businesses either have Inc., Ltd., or Limited in their names.	A less common business entity that is member controlled, and that pools the resources of its members in order to provide products and services to those members.

B. Management Team

There are many different functional roles in an organization that require management. In many start-ups, the entrepreneur holds all of those roles. A bigger organization, however, is divided up into a number of different departments. For example, a product-development team is responsible for coming up with new products and services to market. A marketing team is responsible for coming up with ways to promote products and services to pull customers in. The sales team is responsible for making products and services available for purchase, for pushing products out to customers, and for closing deals. An operations team is responsible for actually running the operations of the business. And the finance team is responsible for making sure funds are available to finance product-development ideas, marketing projects, and daily operations. All of these teams require management.

For each member of your management team, provide a biography that emphasizes relevant experience and expertise. Key areas to highlight include previous titles and positions, domain expertise and market experience, and any outside training or networking connections that may help validate the business plan. Bankers and investors read hundreds of business plans, so the Management and Organization section of your plan is a core component that will be put under a microscope when you send out a funding request.

Titles must reflect the nature of your business. Calling yourself the CEO of a one-person start-up might be inappropriate, but calling yourself the president of a three-person team is fine. Be sure to use the language of your industry by adding relevant titles where necessary, such as a chief technology officer for a tech start-up, or a chief compliance officer for a financial services firm. The titles you use in your company are up to you, but here are some of the traditional titles used in established businesses that you can modify for own your own purposes:

- **President:** The key decision maker in your business. This person is responsible for getting things done, which doesn't necessarily mean doing them alone. The more a president can delegate to an actual or virtual team of managers and/or staff, the more he or she is free to bring revenue to the business.
- **Vice-President of Product Development:** Responsible for researching, developing, and testing new product, technology, or service ideas to increase revenue. This role involves adding new features or improving current features of your products and services.

- **Vice-President of Operations (or Chief Operating Officer):** Responsible for the daily operation of the business. This role may involve managing the processes involved in creating your product or delivering your service, controlling quality, controlling inventory, or fulfilling orders.
- **Vice-President of Marketing (or Chief Marketing Officer):** Responsible for promoting and distributing your product, technology, or service to the market.
- **Vice-President of Sales (or Sales Director):** Responsible for generating and closing sales.
- **Vice-President of Finance (or Chief Financial Officer):** Responsible for making sure your operation is funded, funds are managed, and profits are retained or distributed according to plan.
- **Controller:** Responsible for recording transactions and reporting on the company's annual performance. This role may overlap with the vice president of finance.

C. Advisory Board (and/or Board of Directors)

Advisory Board

What happens when someone with no prior business experience builds a company that starts growing quickly? They run into all kinds of challenges along the way, such as how to hire a management team, when to seek outside investment capital, how to deal with staffing issues, and how to fill the orders that keep coming in. That's where an advisory board comes in. Advisory boards are made up of paid or unpaid business owners, industry experts, and subject-matter experts who act as sounding boards for your business ideas. Investors and banks like to see that you have access to people who can fill your management gaps with periodic advice and feedback. The right advisory board members can bring credibility to your business plan and can connect you with their own network of experts. And that's the role of an advisory board in your business plan.

Whether to pay advisory board members or not is another question. Most start-ups can't afford to pay a team of outside advisers to act as sounding boards. So start with an unpaid advisory board made of people who will speak with you on the phone for an agreed-upon amount of time—such as half an hour per week. Then you could pay them a small fee to give them an incentive to attend quarterly or annual face-to-face meetings or lunches with the entire board present. Just be clear on your goal of getting real advice. Be selective of whom you choose. Seek legal advice to establish a confidentiality agreement that includes straight-forward terms of your relationship. And look for people who can provide guidance, connections, and the ability to make your business look credible in a business plan. Remember, they can't fire you, so choose people who will be both brutally honest and provide competent advice at the same time.

Board of Directors

You might also be required to set up a board of directors if you are seeking substantial funding from outside investors. While management runs your company, a board of directors runs your management—by definition, a board of directors is the group of people who have authority over the management team of a company. They are put in place to appoint management team members, to help set company policy, and to make other general business decisions. Though they are legally bound to your corporation, their authority ends where management decision making begins.

Your board of directors can be made up of a group of outside experts who provide their expertise and support on an as-needed basis. It may also include investors who demand board representation in exchange for their investment capital. If you plan on having a board of directors, discuss their backgrounds and why they have been appointed to your board.

To further reinforce the credibility of your business plan, include each board member's name, credentials, equity position, and required compensation. If available, also include his or her resume.

D. Professional Support

A team is a permanent mix of internal and external generalists, specialists, and subject-matter experts who fill roles in your business. Many roles need to be filled on a full- or part-time basis. Other gaps can be filled by temporary external professionals who perform these roles until your business can afford to bring them in on a full-time basis. An estimate of costs for these outside professionals should be included in your business plan. External support may include:

- **CFO Services:** These are controllers who work two or more hours a week, month, or quarter to do your bookkeeping and ongoing performance and tax reporting.

- **Legal Advisers:** Business lawyers who work on retainer to provide you with as-needed contract, copyright, or business set-up advice.
- **Business Consultants:** Subject-matter expert consultants in your industry who can provide as-needed coaching advice to guide you through the various business challenges that you encounter on your quest. Examples include marketing consultants who can develop seasonal ad campaigns for you without the cost of a full-time marketing director, and process consultants who can help you eliminate time and cost in your operations.

E. Hiring Needs

Every business has different hiring needs. If you start a restaurant, you may require a full team from day one. If you start a product-oriented business, you may outsource most of your work, and only require staff on a periodic basis. In this section of your business plan, include a brief discussion of the employees that you will need to hire, and the total payroll that you will need to fund. Also, if your business will require a layer of management with a line of staff, consider adding an organizational chart. At a minimum, include a table that shows the following:

- **Number of Employees:** The total number of full- and part-time staff in Years 1, 2, and 3.
- **Wages and Salaries:** Total staff wages.
- **Total Payroll:** The total cost of employees, including wages and salaries (including management salaries), and benefits for Years 1, 2, and 3.

DRAGON LORE

Think like an entrepreneur by constantly evolving your business model. Execute like a manager by flawlessly implementing a proven business strategy.

If you want to bolster your pitch to an investor, then highlight the backgrounds of the team members involved in your business. Deep industry experience shows an investor that you have the ability and the experience to achieve success in your sector. When the team from PowerDent Pulse pitched on *Dragons' Den*, they brought four decades of dental industry experience to their pitch, and this background helped them secure a deal.

POWERDENT PULSE

Pitchers: Dr. John Miller, Jim Harrison, and Ali Khonsari, Season 5, Episode 20

BUSINESS MODEL

The company designs and sells power denture brushes.

PROBLEM

Denture wearers complain about how dirty their dentures get and how hard they are to clean. Some research says that only 12% of a denture is actually cleaned when a manual brush is used.

SOLUTION

The first power dual-headed denture brush in the world.

GO-TO-MARKET

The denture aisle in the United States sells about $350 million worth of denture products a year. The pitchers plan to market their power brush through retailers across Canada and the United States.

TEAM

The team has deep experience in the dental industry. Founder Jim Harrison is a denturist, Dr. John Miller is a dentist, and Ali Khonsari owns a dental laboratory.

FINANCIALS

The Ask: $200,000 for 10% equity in the company

Company Valuation: $2,000,000

Current-Year Revenue Projection: 500 units sold to date, plus 4,500 units pending at $39 retail

The Deal: $200,000 for 20%, contingent on the Dragon securing a deal through his industry contacts (He offered to call three potential licensors to see if there was a market for the product. If one of these proved successful, the Dragon wanted 20% of whatever deal is secured.)

Pitchers John Miller, Jim Harrison, and Ali Khonsari presenting their product.

SELF-STUDY WORKSHOP: Management and Organization

For this section of your business plan, draft your talking points first by answering the relevant questions below. Then weave your answers together into a paragraph or two, using bullet points when necessary, and tables or diagrams if appropriate for each of A, B, C, D, and E.

MANAGEMENT AND ORGANIZATION

Overview
A. Business Organization
B. Management Team
C. Advisory Board
D. Professional Support
E. Hiring Needs

OVERVIEW

HR Strategy: What is your human resources strategy?
Talent Pool: Where do you find your talent pool?
Training: What training is required for people to work for you?

Working Environment: What is the culture of your business? What values are important to you in your work? Is it a formal or informal working environment?

Plan Write-Up: *Weave your answers together into a paragraph.*

A. BUSINESS ORGANIZATION

Location: Where is your business (to be) located?

Legal Form of Business: What type of entity is your business?

- ❏ Sole Proprietorship
- ❏ Partnership
- ❏ Corporation
- ❏ Co-operative

Ownership: How is your ownership currently structured? Who owns your business and in what percentages?

Licenses and Permits: What types of licenses and permits have you secured, or do you need to secure?

Plan Write-Up: *Weave your answers together into a paragraph, using bullet points when necessary.*

B. MANAGEMENT TEAM

Key Personnel: Who is responsible for running your business, and what is their job title? Who is responsible for sales and marketing, and what is their job title? Who is responsible for finance, and what is their job title?

Plan Write-Up: *Weave your answers together into a paragraph, using bullet points when necessary.*

C. ADVISORY BOARD

In what areas of your business (finance, marketing, strategy) will you require unpaid third-party advice from time to time?

Who in your circle of influence works, or has worked, in marketing who would be willing to serve on your advisory board? Make sure they don't currently work for one of your competitors.

Who do you know who works, or has worked, in finance who would be willing to serve on your advisory board?

Who do you know who owns a successful business who would be willing to serve on your advisory board?

Make contact with those people who might serve on your advisory board, and ask them if they would be willing to serve.

Plan Write-Up: Weave your answers together into a paragraph, using bullet points when necessary.

D. PROFESSIONAL SUPPORT

Tax Advice: Who will help you with bookkeeping or tax advice?

Legal Advice: Who will provide you with legal advice?

Insurance: Who will provide you with business insurance?

Plan Write-Up: Weave your answers together into a paragraph, using bullet points when necessary.

E. HIRING NEEDS

Employees: How many employees will you need to run your business?

Payroll: What is the total payroll that you will require to meet your objectives in the first three years of business?

HUMAN RESOURCES PLAN

Employee Information	Year 1	Year 2	Year 3
Number of Employees			
Management Salaries			
Staff Wages			
Total Payroll			

Plan Write-Up: *This section consists of a chart only.*

In this chapter, we discussed your plan for managing and staffing your business. In the next chapter, we'll discuss how to put together the financial plan that you will use to fund your operations.

PART V

HOW TO CREATE THE FINANCIAL PLAN

Summarize your projected profit and loss, start-up capital required, and break-even point for the business; how you will use the funds; and your exit strategy.

Chapter 18

How Will You Fund Your Plan?

"This is a PR issue. This isn't an advertising issue. You are absolutely at the tipping point of where the industry is headed and what people want."
—Dragon to Pitcher

SECTION 8: FINANCIAL PLAN

Summarize the highlights of your financial plan. Discuss your projected income and expenses. Identify the amount of investor capital that you are requesting, and explain how you will use it. Identify the companies that might acquire your business in the future.

Lewis Urry invented the alkaline battery that allows us to power our mobile electronics. Marcellus Gilmore Edson invented a patented process for making peanut butter so we can all consume peanuts without having to chew them[1]. James Naismith invented basketball so kids could have an indoor game to play in the winter. And Norman Breakey invented the paint roller so we can all paint our walls faster. All of these inventors were Canadians who made huge contributions to their respective industries.

The difference between then and now is that, had they introduced their inventions today, they would probably be household names. They would have a business plan, an investor pitch, and a shiny logo, and hopefully they'd soon have a lineup of investors. When it comes to your business, if you have significant revenue, a great product, and a confident investor pitch, the odds are high that you will attract capital—even if it's just from a family member or a friend. And if you're fortunate enough to find a strategic investor, you'll have both cash and someone who can balance out the weaknesses in your business plan. The team from Prairie Berries Inc. came to the Dragons' Den with impressive sales, a business loss on their books, and no marketing resources, but they left with a deal from a Dragon who clearly understands the power of a strategic investment.

PRAIRIE BERRIES INC.

Pitchers: Sandra Purdy and Allison Ozog, Season 5, Episode 4

Focus: Attract Capital for Your Business

> "Every day we expose ourselves to environmental stresses, and these stresses can expose ourselves to free-radical production. The free radicals result in cellular damage, which can increase our risk for diseases such as cancer, arthritis, and premature aging. Antioxidants that come in foods like 'Saskatoons' [berries that look like blueberries], reduce the risks of these diseases. We want to be the Ocean Spray of North America."
>
> —Pitcher to Dragons

PRODUCT DESCRIPTION

Berries commonly called "Saskatoon berries" that are naturally high in antioxidants.

DRAGONS' DEN BY THE NUMBERS

- **The Ask:** $250,000 for 49.9% equity in the company
- **Company Valuation:** $501,002
- **The Deal:** $250,000 in marketing services (includes $50,000 in cash) in exchange for a 10% royalty on any incremental business
- **1:** The number of advertisements that one Dragon feels the pitcher would be able to buy with $250,000
- **$389,000:** Sales to date
- **$64,000:** The loss the business was generating before receiving funding

Pitchers Sandra Purdy and Allison Ozog preparing to give the Dragons a taste of their Saskatoon berry juice.

SECTION 8: FINANCIAL PLAN

The financial plan section of your business plan describes how you plan to finance your venture and how you expect it to perform. It summarizes your projected profit and loss, start-up capital requirements, and the future assets of the business. It also shows an investor your break-even point, sources and uses of cash, and your exit strategy for the business and/ or its investors.

If you are not comfortable with business finance, at least do the research in the workshop at the end of this chapter. Then seek outside assistance from someone like an accountant or business consultant. This will allow you to direct your energy toward the most important part of your business—establishing a profitable and sustainable business model. The financial section of your business plan is one that investors or banks will go through with a fine-tooth comb, so seek outside assistance if you lack experience in this area. The following are the sections to include in your financial plan:

A. **Financial Summary:** Financial highlights, assumptions, and projected profit and loss summary.
B. **Financing Details**: Funding request, capitalization table, and exit strategy.

C. **Financial Performance:** Income statement, balance sheet, cash-flow statement, and ratio analysis.

D. **Risk and Mitigation:** The risk that your business venture faces and how you plan to mitigate it.

A. Financial Summary

Having a clear picture of your financial position at all times can mean the difference between having a sustainable business and one that suddenly runs out of capital. If you don't have a system in place for tracking sales, costs, and accounts receivable, you risk thinking that your business is doing better than it is. Financial controls should be put in place early, including a bookkeeping process that tracks expenses and a performance-reporting system for updating your financial statements monthly, quarterly, and annually so you always know where your business stands. It's also wise to assume that investors or lenders may not have time to read your financial statements to find what they are looking for, so in this opening section of your financial plan, provide a brief summary of your financials in four key areas:

- **Revenue:** Revenue targets for the next three to five years.
- **Profit:** Projected profit margin for each of the next three to five years.
- **Assumptions:** Assumptions you have made with respect to the costs of your business.
- **Break-Even Point:** The revenue you need to generate per month in order to cover your costs.

Break-Even Analysis

The total number of units of your product or service that have to be sold to break even on your fixed costs is called your break-even point. These are not hard-and-fast rules, but you can have a break-even for a weekly, monthly, or annual period, or a time to pay back an initial capital outlay for a business. That's why some investors request a royalty until their initial capital investment is recouped, and take a percentage of equity thereafter. You can calculate a break-even in many different ways, including the break-even that covers your design and set-up costs, a break-even to cover your business start-up costs, or the monthly break-even on your entire business to cover your monthly operating costs. Here are two methods for calculating a break-even point:

Method 1:

Monthly Break-Even = [Total Fixed Costs]/[Per-unit Gross Profit*]
   *can be a unit of time, a project, a unit of product/service.

Method 2:

Payback Period = [Total Capital Investment]/[Annual Cash Flow to Investor]

B. Financing Details

Funding Request

Some people might ask you why you need outside capital, if you have such a great business idea. The answer is that many opportunities require investments up front that put you in a position to capitalize on them. In this section of your financial plan, you should state how much capital you are requesting, and then explain the planned uses of the funds being requested, which could include the following:

- **Working Capital:** Working capital is needed to pay for the day-to-day operations of your business, including marketing costs, payroll, inventory, and other operating expenses. Banks and investors will look to see if you are able to generate sufficient cash flow to cover your working-capital needs, and, if not, when you'll be able to do so.
- **Growth Capital:** Growth capital is needed to fund new marketing initiatives or capital items, such as equipment, that you need in order to take advantage of a sales opportunity or cost reductions. In most cases, banks and investors will assume that it will take more than one year for your business to generate enough cash flow to cover your cash-flow expenses.

Capitalization Table

A capitalization table (a.k.a. *cap table*) shows the current ownership structure of your business by percentage. If you have existing investors, list each investor and the percentage of your business that each currently owns.

Exit Strategy

When you first start your business, the last thing you are thinking about is when you are going to shut down or sell it. Even if you have pie-in-the-sky dreams of running your business until you're 90 years old, you should still set it up so it can operate without you present. And that makes it saleable. One of the benefits of seeing your business through a planning lens, with a clear exit strategy, is that it obligates you to make your operations efficient enough to run without you. Having the ability to leave any time also gives the start-up entrepreneur and investors the peace of mind of knowing that they are not dependent on the entrepreneur's presence.

In this section of your financial plan, tell investors and banks when their investment or loan will show a return. Some of the more well-known, yet not necessarily most common, exits, or "liquidity events," for a business are the following:

- **Acquisition or Sale:** A third party buys your business and you distribute the proceeds of sale according to an advance agreement. This option is a true exit from the business in that you sell your ownership to someone else and step away from it. In this section, list three to five companies that may potentially buy your business and why.
- **Share Buyback:** You agree in advance to purchase investors' shares back at a stipulated date in the future. This option can drain a company's capital because cash will have to be found at the appropriate time.
- **Royalty Payback:** Payment of a royalty to an investor until the investor receives his or her money back, with a percentage of equity in the business thereafter.
- **Initial Public Offering:** You sell shares in your business to the public on a stock exchange. This option can provide current investors with liquidity, while not draining the capital of the company. This process is so complex and unlikely, that putting it in your business plan as a potential exit could damage the credibility of your plan.

C. Financial Performance
Income Statement: Financial Performance
The purpose of an income statement (a.k.a. profit and loss statement, or P&L) is to measure the performance of your business over a specific time period, such as the next three to five years. Also include a three-year historical statement if you already have sales.

Be aware that this statement has nothing to do with cash flow. A business might have $500,000 in positive cash flow this year because an investor has written a cheque for that amount, but that doesn't make your business profitable. At the same time, a business might appear to be profitable, but could go under at any minute because much of that profit might be tied up in accounts receivable. That's because various non-cash revenue and expenses (accounts receivable, depreciation expense, etc.) can make a business look profitable, but if it is lacking actual cash, the business may not have enough money to pay its bills.

Ideally, you should put a rough draft of your financial statements together yourself first. Then if you have any questions or concerns about formatting or strategy, you can always seek assistance from a local accountant or business adviser for one or two hours of their time. Start with a rough a list of expenses in Years 1, 2, and 3. The following are the components of an income statement:

- **Sales:** Revenue from the sale of your products, or the performance of your services.
- **Cost of Goods Sold:** The amount you pay for goods for resale, raw materials, and labour to produce your product—the inputs required to perform your service.
- **Gross Profit:** Refers to profit on the goods and services you sell before overhead (selling, general, and administrative expenses) is taken into account.
- **Operating Expenses:** Refers to the selling, general, and administrative expenses you incur to sell your products and services (for example, sales commissions) and administer your business (rent, utilities, office salaries, office supplies, insurance, licenses, etc.).
- **Net Income from Operations (EBITDA*):** Pre-tax and pre-interest profit of the business. (*EBITDA can be used in place of operating income if there is no other income coming into the business.)
- **Net Income before Taxes:** Pre-tax and post-interest profit of the business.
- **Net Income after Taxes:** Post-tax and post-interest profit of the business.

Balance Sheet: Financial Condition

A balance sheet is a formatted list of your assets, liabilities (debts), and owners' equity. A business plan should include a single-year balance sheet. If your business has significant assets and liabilities, then consider putting in a three- to five-year projected balance sheet. The purpose of a balance sheet is to report the financial condition of your business at a specific point in time. It's called a balance sheet because it's based on a simple formula:

$$Assets = Liabilities + Owners' Equity$$

In simple terms, if you own more than you owe, your business is healthy, although "healthy" is a relative term because unforeseen obligations, such as a lawsuit, could impair your ability to do business in the future. For a single-year balance sheet, your assets and their dollar values are listed on the left side of the sheet, and your debts and owners' equity are listed on the right side of the sheet. The components of a balance sheet include:

Assets
- **Current Assets:** Most liquid assets, such as cash equivalents, accounts receivable, inventories, prepaid expenses, and other assets that can be converted into cash within one year or less. These are assets you don't intend to keep for more than one year (other than cash).
- **Fixed Assets:** Land, buildings and equipment, furniture, and fixtures that you intend to keep for more than one year. These are assets you don't intend to sell within the next year because they typically last for more than one year.

Liabilities
- **Current Liabilities:** Bills that are due in one year or less. This may include short-term loans and accounts payable.
- **Long-Term Debt:** Debt that doesn't need to be paid in full within the next year. Long-term debt eventually becomes a current liability in the year it comes due. This may include a bank loan for your business, a car loan, or a mortgage on a building you have bought.

Equity (What is left for the owners of a company after all of the debts have been paid.)
- **Owners' Investment:** Refers to the amount of money or property that has been contributed to your business by the investors. For some companies, this may include classes of stock such as common or preferred stock.
- **Retained Earnings:** The undistributed profits that you decide to keep in your business. Most capital-intensive companies retain profits in their business in order to fund future projects, replace equipment, or invest in future opportunities.

Cash-Flow Statement: Cash Position

A business survives on cash, not accounts receivable. If a customer agrees to buy from you now, but pays you later, that can put serious pressure on your ability to pay any of your suppliers, vendors, and employees who need to be paid in the interim. That's why it's important to include a 12-month cash-flow statement for Year 1. Also include an annualized cash-flow statement for Years 1 to 5 if your cash-flow statement differs significantly from your income statement.

A cash-flow statement is a list of the total cash coming into your business and cash going out within a set period of time. Any time you can show positive cash flow, you'll draw favour from investors and banks when they review your plan. There are three types of cash flow:

- **Operating Cash Flows:** Incoming cash revenue, and outgoing cash payments to pay your bills.
- **Investing Cash Flows:** Incoming cash flows from the sale of old equipment, and outgoing cash flows to buy new equipment.
- **Financing Cash Flows:** Cash injections or loans from investors or banks, as well as cash payments you make back to them.

Banks will want to know that you can cover the loan payments due to them. Investors will want to know that you are contributing to profit with actual cash flow (not just accounts receivable that may or may not come to fruition). To build a cash-flow statement, understand three key phrases:

- **Cash Inflows:** You may receive financing cash from investors or banks, cash from sales, or cash from the sale of old equipment.
- **Cash Outflows:** You'll disburse cash to pay for staffing needs and salaries, taxes, equipment purchases, inventory purchases, and to make monthly debt payments.
- **Burn Rate:** The rate at which you use up investor capital.

Ratio Analysis

Ratios help you and interested investors or bankers understand how healthy your business venture is, or will be in the future. They also help you compare the financial health of your business to industry standards. Ratios are simple to calculate once you have built your income statement or balance sheet. They are calculated by creating relationships between two or more items from a balance sheet and/or an income statement.

Profitability ratios tell investors and banks how profitable your business is, and, in turn, how profitable their own return will be.

PROFITABILITY RATIOS

Net Profit Margin	Return on Investment	Return on Equity
profit *divided by* sales	profit *divided by* total investment	pre-tax profit *divided by* owners' equity

Liquidity ratios tell investors and banks whether you can meet your financial obligations when they come due.

LIQUIDITY RATIOS

Current Ratio	Quick Ratio	Inventory Turnover Ratio
current assets *divided by* current liabilities	current assets-inventory *divided by* current liabilities	cost of goods sold (COGS) *divided by* average inventory in stock

Debt ratios tell investors and banks how leveraged your business is compared to established industry norms.

DEBT RATIOS

Debt-to-Equity Ratio	Times Interest Earned
long term debt *divided by* owners' equity	profit *divided by* interest expense

D. Risk and Mitigation

Investors want to know the truth about your business. Part of that comes from being transparent about the potential risks that you are facing. Being open about risk shows that you know your business, and this level of honesty could actually add to the credibility of your business plan if you discuss how you plan to mitigate those risks. The types of risk that you should cover in this section of your business plan include:

- **Liability Risk:** The risk of being sued.
- **Market Risk:** The risk of a sudden market shift, or new competitors entering the market.
- **Operational Risk:** The risks of operating your business, such as losing a supplier, or being understaffed.

- **Financial Risk:** How leveraged your business is, and the risk of investors pulling out of the company or loans being called.
- **Regulatory Risk:** The risk of being regulated out of business.

DRAGON LORE

Every time you receive investment capital, you reduce your equity percentage in your business. Be sure to fully understand how new investment capital will dilute your position in your business.

If your business proposal to investors gets turned down, it doesn't necessarily mean that you don't have a good business. If your venture is profitable enough to cover all of your costs, and provide you with an adequate salary, then from a financial standpoint, that is certainly enough to keep you in business. Pitcher Julie Arora of Mom's Healthy Secrets came to the Dragons' Den with $600,000 in revenue, and a 10% profit after her salary. And though she left without a deal in hand, she knew enough about her numbers and the value of her proposal to reject a deal from a very wealthy investor.

MOM'S HEALTHY SECRETS

Pitcher: Julie Arora, Season 6, Episode 16

BUSINESS MODEL

The company sells healthy, functional cereal for $6 a box at major grocery chains throughout Canada. According to Health Canada, a functional food is a food that is "consumed as part of a usual diet, and is demonstrated to have [health] benefits and/or reduce the risk of chronic disease beyond basic nutritional functions."[2]

PROBLEM

Major cereal manufacturers are concerned with their profit margins, and not always with the health of their customers. This means that many breakfast cereals have very little nutritional value.

SOLUTION

A healthy breakfast cereal that is loaded with fibre and antioxidants.

GO-TO-MARKET

The company sells the product through major chains across Canada. The pitcher wants to extend her line with six new healthy cereals, including hot cereals and pancake mix.

TEAM

Pitcher Julie Arora used her mom's secret recipes to launch her line.

FINANCIALS

The Ask: $100,000 for 10% of the company
Company Valuation: $1 million
Company Revenue: $600,000 last year, with a 10% profit after owner's salary
The Deal: $0 (the pitcher turned down an offer of $100,000 for 40% of the company)

Pitcher Julie Arora turning down a $100,000 deal from a Dragon.

SELF-STUDY WORKSHOP: Financial Plan

For this section of your business plan, draft your talking points first by answering the relevant questions below. Then weave your answers together into a paragraph or two, using bullet points when necessary, and tables or diagrams if appropriate for each of A through D.

FINANCIAL PLAN

A. Financial Summary
B. Financing Details
C. Financial Performance
D. Risk and Mitigation

A. FINANCIAL SUMMARY

Highlights: What are the highlights of your financial plan?
Revenue: What revenue do you expect to achieve in Years 1, 2, and 3?
Break-Even: How many units of your product or service do you need to sell to break even on a monthly basis?
Return on Investment: How long will it take to recoup or pay back your initial investment?
Profit: When will your business turn a profit?
Assumptions: In order to achieve your profit targets, what assumptions have you made with respect to cost of goods sold, operating expenses, interest, tax, supplier terms, etc.?
Capital: What amount of capital are you seeking?
Plan Write-Up: *Weave your answers together into a paragraph, using bullet points when necessary. Insert a graph of your three- to five-year financial highlights, plus the last three years if you have them.*

FINANCIAL OVERVIEW

Financial Metric	Year 1	Year 2	Year 3	Year 4	Year 5
Revenue					
Cost of Goods					
Gross Margin					
Operating Expenses*					
EBITDA					

*excluding interest, tax, depreciation & amortization

B. FINANCING DETAILS

Funding Request: How much capital are you requesting from investors?
Working Capital Uses: How will you use the working capital? List how much capital you will allocate to each of the following:

- Inventory
- Marketing Costs
- Staff
- Other

Growth Capital Uses: How will you use the growth capital? List how much capital you will allocate to each of the following:

- Building
- Equipment
- Furniture & Fixtures
- Other

CAPITALIZATION TABLE

Investor	Date	Investment	Shares	Ownership
Common				
Preferred				
Totals				100%

Exit Strategy: How will the investor get his or her money back? In this section, mention potential acquirers, a share buy-back, royalty, merger, or other liquidity event that could cash out the investor in the future.

Plan Write-Up: *Weave your answers together into a paragraph, using bullet points when necessary.*

C. FINANCIAL PERFORMANCE

Income Statement: Create an income statement that shows your projected income, expenses, and profit for the next three to five years.

INCOME STATEMENT (OR P&L STATEMENT)

	Year 1	Year 2	Year 3	Year 4	Year 5
REVENUE					
Sales (A)					
Direct Labour Cost (B)					
Direct Material Cost (C)					
COGS	= B + C				
Gross Profit (D)	D = A − (B + C)				
Less: EXPENSES					
Advertising & Promotion					
Car & Truck Expenses					
Commission & Fees					
Contract Labour					
Depreciation & Amortization					
Employee Benefits					
Insurance					
Legal & Professional Fees					
Office Expenses					
Rent or Lease					
Repairs & Maintenance					
Supplies					
Licenses & Permits					
Travel, Meals & Entertainment					
Utilities					
Salaries & Wages*					
Other Expenses (Storage, Freight, etc.)					
Total Expenses (E)					
Net Income from Operations	= D − E				
Less: Interest Expense					

(Continued)

	Year 1	Year 2	Year 3	Year 4	Year 5
Net Income Before Taxes					
Less: Tax Expense					
Net Income/Loss					

*Selling, general, and administrative salaries and wages. Any wages paid to make the product are included in the cost of goods sold (COGS) section.

Balance Sheet: Create a balance sheet that shows the projected assets, debts, and owners' equity in your business for one year (or for the next three to five years, if assets and liabilities are significant).

BALANCE SHEET

	Year 1	Year 2	Year 3	Year 4	Year 5
ASSETS					
Current Assets					
Cash					
Accounts Receivable					
Inventory					
Prepaid Expenses					
Total Current Assets					
Fixed Assets					
Land					
Buildings					
Depreciation Offset					
Equipment					
Depreciation Offset					
Furniture & Fixtures					
Autos & Vehicles					
Other Assets					
Total Fixed Assets					
TOTAL ASSETS					

	Year 1	Year 2	Year 3	Year 4	Year 5
LIABILITIES					
Current Liabilities					
Accounts Payable					
Short-Term Debt					
Accrued Liabilities					
Other Current Liabilities					
Total Current Liabilities					
Long-Term Liabilities					
Long-Term Debt					
Other Liabilities					
Total Long-Term Liabilities					
EQUITY					
Owners' Investment					
Retained Earnings					
Total Equity					
TOTAL LIABILITIES & EQUITY					

Cash-Flow Statement: Create a cash-flow statement that shows your projected cash receipts, disbursements, and net cash flow for the next 12 months (or for the next three to five years if your cash flows differ significantly from your income statement).

MONTHLY CASH-FLOW STATEMENT

	1	2	3	4	5	6	7	8	9	10	11	12
Cash Inflows												
Cash Sales												
Receivables Paid												
Loan Proceeds												
Invested Capital												
Other Cash Receipts												
Total Cash Inflows												

(Continued)

	1	2	3	4	5	6	7	8	9	10	11	12
Cash Outflows												
Cash COGS												
Cash Operating Expenses												
Cash Purchases												
Loan Payments												
Investor Payback												
Owners' Draw												
Taxes Paid												
Other Disbursements												
Total Cash Outflows												
Net Cash Flow												

Ratio Analysis: Using the income statement and balance sheet, calculate the ratios for your business using the formulas explained earlier in this chapter.

RATIO ANALYSIS

	Year 1	Year 2	Year 3	Year 4	Year 5
Profitability					
Net Profit Margin					
Return on Investment					
Return on Equity					
Liquidity					
Current Ratio					
Quick Ratio					
Inventory Turnover Ratio					
Debt					
Debt-to-Equity					
Time Interest Earned					

Plan Write-Up: *No write-up is required for your financial statements and ratio chart, since you have summarized them elsewhere. Just include the charts you have produced here.*

D. RISK AND MITIGATION

Liability Risks: What liability risks does your business face? Why would someone sue you?

Market Risks: What market risks does your business face? What market factor or new competitor could put you out of business?

Regulatory Risks: What regulatory risks does your business face? What current or new regulations could hinder your ability to do business?

Operating Risks: What operating risks does your business face? What supply or staffing shortages could hurt your business?

Financial Risks: What financial risks does your business face?

Other Risks: What other risks does your business face?

Mitigation: What steps are you taking to mitigate these risks? (For example, insurance, patents, HR policies, terms of trade, etc.)

Plan Write-Up: *Weave your answers together into one or two paragraphs with bullet points when necessary.*

The financial section of your business plan, the last section, is arguably the make or break section of your plan. If you have a wonderful business idea, but the financials don't show that you and your investors can achieve their goals, then you might need to change your business model. In the next section, we'll discuss a supporting document for your business plan called the Operations Plan. The Operations Plan describes how you plan to operate your business on a day-to-day basis, complete with the process you will follow to actually produce and deliver your product or service.

PART VI

HOW TO OPERATIONALIZE YOUR BUSINESS

Describe your operating model and how you are prepared to handle sudden increases in order volume.

CHAPTER 19

OPERATIONALIZE YOUR PLAN

"What's missing in the whole presentation was how to bring it to market. I don't want to solve the marketing problem. I just want to write you a cheque and say, 'When is it coming back times three?' You don't know how to go sell it."
— Dragon to Pitcher

APPENDIX: Operations Plan

Define your operating processes and staffing needs. Eliminate inefficient or costly steps. Refine your process over time to eliminate unnecessary steps.

Most businesses have their roots in operational simplicity. Dennis Wilson started Lululemon Athletica with one store in Vancouver, British Columbia, and grew it into a multi-store corporation that has hundreds of millions of dollars in revenue. Frank C. Mars started selling confectionery from his kitchen, and his family company grew into one of the largest confectionery companies in the world. Steve Wozniak and Steve Jobs built the first Apple computers at Steve Jobs's house, and today the company is worth more than Microsoft on the stock market. Over time, the simplicity of producing and selling a single product, or running a single store, becomes overwhelmed by the complexity of an operation that needs layers of management to function well.

After you have communicated in your business plan that you have an investable product or service, the next step is to demonstrate that you know how to produce it. This part of your business plan is called an operations plan. While investor-ready business plans generally don't include a detailed operations plan, a full business plan does. Your operations plan describes the daily processes you will follow to create value for your customers, and the assets required to make those processes possible. It identifies your production or service-delivery processes, facilities, raw materials, staff and equipment, packaging, quality control, inventory control, order fulfillment, and customer service. In a nutshell, it demonstrates to investors that you can not only plan your business, but you can also operate it.

Once you nail down a successful operating model, you might just find that investors aren't merely willing to invest in your business—they might be ready to buy it. When Carolanne Doig of Seaforth Rain Gear visited *Dragons' Den*, she put her successful business before herself and ended up with an offer from one Dragon for 100% of her business.

SEAFORTH RAIN GEAR

Pitcher: Carolanne Doig, Season 5, Episode 16

Focus: A Successful Operating Model

"Although I have over 90% of the players using it, and about 96% of the players on the LPGA tour, I actually have never paid anyone to use it . . . *they* phone *me*. I've put a lot into this, but I'm ready to let someone else take the wheel and drive this car. I really have more faith in the product than I have in myself. So I would like you to invest in this so that we can take this product to the next level."
—Pitcher to Dragons

PRODUCT DESCRIPTION

A line of golf rain gear.

DRAGONS' DEN BY THE NUMBERS

- **The Ask:** $100,000 for 40% equity in the company
- **Company Valuation:** $250,000
- **The Deal:** $200,000 for 100% of the company and all relevant patents, plus 5% royalty to be paid back to the pitcher on all sales for the next five years, contingent on the Dragon speaking to colleagues in the golf industry to establish whether there is any distribution available for the product
- **$200,000:** Prior-year sales

- **96%:** Percentage of players on the PGA and LPGA tours who use the rain hood
- **$20–$25:** The price of rain hats and gloves
- **7:** The number of ounces that the Seaforth rain hood weighs
- **14:** The number of years Carolanne has been in business

Carolanne Doig describing how she has over 90% of players on the PGA and LPGA tours using her Seaforth products.

THE WARM-UP: OPERATIONS PLAN DEFINED

An operations plan is a description of how you plan to make your product or deliver your service. The purpose of an operations plan is to demonstrate that you are prepared to operate your business and produce your product in a scalable and repeatable manner. The sections of an operations plan include:

A. **Location**
B. **Process Map and Staffing**
C. **Equipment, Supplies, and Packaging**
D. **Order Fulfillment, Billing, and Customer Service**
E. **Controls**

A. Location

A business can only operate as fast as its slowest bottleneck. If you don't plan properly, the location and layout of your business can lead to a serious drop in the overall sales and employee productivity of your business. Lack of planning in location and layout can not only lead to downtime, but can also lead to serious space limitations later on. If you have no experience in layout or location considerations, think about hiring a consultant to help you design your floor space to meet the needs of your business. Or, do some research through your industry or trade association into how related tasks should be organized. Layout strategy is a critical skill that can improve the flow of any operation, whether it's an office, manufacturing facility, or kitchen in a restaurant.

Physical Location

The importance of where your business is located depends on the type of business you are in. A retail outlet is heavily dependent on foot and vehicle traffic. Sam Walton of Walmart used to fly over the off-ramps of highways to watch traffic patterns from the air, in order to figure out where to build his next store. A manufacturer has to be able to source raw materials and ship its product, so auto manufacturers typically locate as close to shipping and transportation arteries as possible. Technology firms are heavily dependent on highly skilled talent pools, which can make or break the quality of the product they put out, so companies like RIM locate near tech corridors like Waterloo, Ontario. And professional service firms that have walk-in client traffic depend on a specific service image, so they aren't typically located in industrial complexes, which might hurt their business image.

In this section of your operations plan, discuss where your business will be located, and how any of the following factors have an impact on your choice:

- **Customers:** How close do you have to be to customers?
- **Talent Pool:** Are you dependent on highly skilled workers, or can you train your staff?
- **Transportation Arteries:** Do you have to be near specific air, ground, or water transportation?
- **Suppliers:** Do you need to be close to suppliers?

Layout

Layout is the arrangement of workstations, inventory, and equipment within your business location. The goal of layout is to maximize the sales volume or worker productivity per square foot of space. In this section of your operations plan, discuss the basic structure, square footage, and layout requirements of your floor space. Include the rationale for your choices, and a sketch, blueprint, or diagram. The role of layout considerations depends on the type of business you are in.

- **Plant Layout:** You can lay out your manufacturing floor space to accommodate workstations where employees complete specific tasks such as sewing, printing, or cutting. Or, you can set it up like a Henry Ford–style assembly line, with workstations lined up in sequence, so each step of the process can be quickly followed up with the work of the next workstation. Be sure to include a discussion of the space you require for storage, shipping and receiving, restrooms, and any other specialized needs that must be met.
- **Retail Layout:** You can map out your retail location with an aisle or aisles that lead the customer in a circular fashion. Or you can use an aisle-less layout where the customer travels aimlessly throughout the store. Your choice can have a big impact on how much sales volume you generate per square foot of retail space. Be sure to include a discussion of whether or not you need space for a workroom, a storage area, shipping and receiving, or a restroom.
- **Office Layout:** You can map out your office space to enhance worker productivity and make the most efficient use of your limited workspace. You can set up an open-concept office with separate work areas, so staff can work together and rapidly share ideas. Or, if privacy is a major concern in your business, you can set up separate, enclosed offices for each individual.

Expansion Plans

Businesses need to plan for growth. Very few business start-ups should consider buying a business location in the early stages. Renting or leasing your space is usually a better alternative because it gives you the flexibility to move or change strategy mid-course if the market suddenly shifts. This is another area where legal advice is critical so that you don't get locked into a lease that doesn't serve your purposes. In this section of your operations plan, discuss how you would accommodate sudden increases in order volume, including where you would store additional materials and finished inventory if your current planned location is not sufficient.

B. Process Map and Staffing

Process Map

A process refers to everything you do to produce your product or provide your service. If you own a manufacturing firm, you might have a job shop that does custom work, or an assembly line that produces widgets. If you own a restaurant, your process entails food and drink preparation. Whether you own a manufacturing firm, own a retail outlet, or work out of an office, it's important to walk through the steps of your process to make sure that you are prepared for the costs and resources involved. In this section of your operations plan, demonstrate to your reader that your operating model is well thought out. Here are some key points to touch on:

- **Capital vs. Labour:** Your business is either labour intensive or capital intensive. Labour intensive means that it takes more labour to produce your product than it does equipment or technology. A landscaping service is an example of a labour-intensive business. Capital intensive means that it takes more equipment and technology to produce your product than it does labour. A computer manufacturer is capital intensive.
- **Capacity:** Your new operation will have the capacity to produce a certain amount of inventory, or serve a certain number of customers. Describe how much volume you will be able to deliver within a certain amount of time, such as a year or week (depending on your business type).
- **Competitive Edge:** Discuss the cost, time, or productivity advantages that your process gives you over the competition.
- **Flow Chart:** A flow chart can help provide a visual summary of the steps involved in your operation. Examples of these steps are "drive nails," "type letters," or "shrink-wrap boxes." After you fill the steps involved into various boxes in your flow chart, you should then add a written description of the raw materials, workers, and time required for each step.

Staffing

Once you have drawn a flow chart for your process, describe who will execute each step. Include both full- and part-time staffing needs for each stage, with projected wages and salaries. Also describe your recruiting process, such as plans for advertising, or for working with job-search firms, staffing companies, and employment agencies. This is where location can come into play. Once your staff projections are in place, include costs for any benefits packages that you'll need in order to retain and motivate employees.

C. Equipment, Supplies, and Packaging

Procurement is the process of buying equipment, supplies, and packaging for your business. The objective of procurement is to not only buy raw materials or goods to sell, but also to find the most fitting quality for the lowest possible price. Be clear about your vendor-selection criteria, such as quality, price, vendor support services, lead time, and references. In this section of your operations plan, describe what you need and how you plan to acquire it in each of the following areas:

- **Equipment:** Your operations plan should include an equipment list. A manufacturing firm might need specialized machinery, trucks, and vehicles, for example. Retail outlets will need cash registers, computers, and security systems. And an office will need a fax machine, printer, and scanner. Put a dollar figure on each piece, and identify how often it will need to be replaced, any capacity limitations of the machine, and how you will maintain and replace it over time.
- **Supplies:** Calculating your cost of goods sold (COGS) is a complex process that involves projecting unit volume, creating a list of components and raw materials, calculating a per-unit cost to produce and store each finished item sold, and adding the cost of ordering and receiving raw materials. In this section of your operations plan, list the supplies you will need to produce your product or deliver your service.
- **Packaging:** Packaging is more than just a container for your product. It can help make your product more convenient to consume, provide protection, and promote your product or service through a unique look and feel. When you think of Mateus wine, Coca-Cola, Heinz Tomato Ketchup, or the iPhone, packaging is a huge part of their brands, and is a big part of the buyer experience. In this section of your operations plan, discuss your packing, per-unit costs, and any specialized labels you will use. Also provide a list of the descriptions, features, benefits, specifications, customer service, directions, price, scanner codes, and company information that you will include on your packaging.

D. Order Fulfillment, Billing, and Customer Service

Fulfillment & Billing

Fulfillment is the process of taking, filling, and tracking orders. Billing is the point of the fulfillment process where the customer actually pays you with cash, a cheque, or a credit card. If you don't make this part of your process easy by using a 1-800 number or e-commerce site, you could end up losing a substantial amount of business to your competition. Every part of this process needs to be planned in detail so that there are no delays between the time an order is placed and the time the customer receives the order. In this section of your operations plan, discuss how the customer pays you, how you fulfill orders— including how you pick-and-pack (for inventory businesses)—and how you ship (Canada Post, courier, or hand delivery). Also describe how you track orders once they have been placed or shipped.

With computer technology, almost every step of this process can be automated to ensure timeliness and accuracy. Speak to your industry or trade association to find software or Web applications that are prepackaged and custom made for your industry. If your order volume is high enough, you might even outsource order fulfillment to a third-party business, so you can focus on your core business. Third-party fulfillment houses can reduce your cost of storage, manage your inventory levels, and physically distribute your goods.

Customer Service

Customer service refers to everything you do to help customers buy, use, maintain, or return your product or service. A great product that is delivered long after its estimated delivery date loses its lustre. A rude or less-than-courteous phone demeanour can overshadow quality products. And an inaccurate order can leave customers flustered enough to cancel their order and request a refund. Dissatisfied customers can be even more damaging to your business than satisfied customers can be good for it. So pay close attention to the customer service element of your business. The following are key components of a sound customer service model:

- **Warranties:** Refunds, replacements, and repairs.
- **Phone Support:** After-sales support to help customers use your products or understand your services. In some cases, this might be fee-based support.

- **Web Support:** Online support through "Frequently Asked Questions" pages, an online knowledge base, or online chats for higher volume businesses.

E. Controls

A control is an important operational tool that allows you to measure your work against pre-established benchmarks. Some controls are internal, such as quality standards, inventory levels, or financial controls. Others are external, such as compliance and regulatory standards. When put in place, controls will tell you when you are doing a good job and when corrective action needs to be taken. In this section of your operations plan, describe any controls you have in place with respect to those listed in the following table:

INTERNAL CONTROLS

Quality Control	Inventory Control	Compliance
Spot checks of your product, process, or customer service to compare quality of output to a pre-set standard. Use checklists to look for defects, and take corrective action when necessary. *Examples include greeting all visitors to your store; having precooked weights for all food; answering the phone within three rings; spot-checking employee work; or even setting up "old school" suggestion boxes to request feedback from customers on written cards.*	Coordinating inventory needs with sales and marketing, creating reorder points, or having backup or safety stock in storage for unexpected sales spikes. Use inventory control to prevent stock-outs, or to minimize the cost of carrying excess inventory. *Examples include using a perpetual counting system by reconciling physical counts of raw materials and finished product against computer figures at regular intervals.*	Self-auditing your business periodically to ensure compliance with provincial or federal regulators. *Examples include spot-checking files for professional service firms; self-inspecting food preparation and storage areas daily for a food business; or self-auditing for compliance with certain ISO standards for a manufacturing firm.*

DRAGON LORE

Focus on the seven to ten steps of your process that create real value for the customer. Increase productivity and cut costs over time by looking for ways to cut unnecessary steps out of the process.

One of the more complex operations to run is a spirits business. The need for a distillery, a source of high-quality water, taste tests, and package development, and the complex process of getting a listing through the government liquor board, can make even the most passionate of entrepreneurs shy away from the business. When John Vellinga of Slava Ultra Premium Vodka entered the Dragons' Den, he had sales and an operation in place to produce and market his product. But that wasn't enough to convince the Dragons to sign a cheque. The fact that Vella had already sunk $2.5 to $3 million of capital on putting the operation in place was a major deal breaker.

SLAVA ULTRA PREMIUM VODKA

Pitcher: John Vellinga, Season 6, Episode 17

BUSINESS MODEL

The pitcher developed a premium vodka from the ground up, and now sells it for $28 per bottle.

PROBLEM

Drinkers want premium vodka without the premium price.

SOLUTION

The only ultra-premium vodka on the market at the $28 price point.

GO-TO-MARKET

Launched through liquor stores across four provinces: Manitoba, Saskatchewan, Alberta, and Ontario.

TEAM

John Vellinga and his wife produce the vodka through a distillery in the Ukraine.

FINANCIALS

The Ask: $500,000 for 5% of the company
Company Valuation: $10 million

Company Revenue: $512,000 last year; projecting over $1 million this year
The Deal: $0

Ultra Premium Slava Vodka being pitched on Dragons' Den.

SELF-STUDY WORKSHOP: Operations Plan

For this section of your business plan, draft your talking points first by answering the relevant questions below. Then weave your answers together into a paragraph or two, bullet points when necessary, and tables or diagrams if appropriate for each of A, B, C, D, and E.

OPERATIONS PLAN

A. Location
B. Process Map and Staffing
C. Equipment, Supplies and Packaging
D. Order Fulfillment, Billing and Customer Service
E. Controls

Begin by summarizing your operating model in a two- to three-sentence opening paragraph.

A. LOCATION

Location: Describe your location. Where is your business located? Why was this location chosen (proximity to customers, suppliers, transportation hubs, etc.)?

Layout: What is special about the layout of your business? What is the square footage of your location, and how much capacity can your business handle through this location?

Expansion Plans: How much capacity can your business handle per square foot of space? Do you require a separate warehouse for inventory, and can warehousing be outsourced? Where can you get additional space if your business outgrows its planned location?

Plan Write-Up: *Weave your answers together into a paragraph, with bullet points when necessary.*

B. PROCESS MAP AND STAFFING

Process Map: Describe your production process or service-delivery process.

Output: What is the output of your production process (for example, a product, a type of service, other)? How many units of product or service are you trying to produce per day, week, month, or some other relevant time interval?

Production Process: What are the main stages of your production process, and how is value added at each stage? Try to boil it down to seven to ten stages, with one short sentence or phrase for each stage. Which stages are outsourced or offshored, if any?

Process Map: For each of your core products or services, produce a process map of the core stages of your production process or service-delivery process. Start by listing the stages of your process, then draw a visual flow chart that represents that process.

Stage	Value Added	Equipment	Labour

Flow Chart: Draw a flow chart (boxes with arrows between them) of the seven to ten main stages of your operating process, with a one- to two-word description for each stage.

Capacity: What is the capacity that you *could* produce or deliver in a day, week, month, or year using this process, if pressured?

Cost: What is the total cost to produce one unit (i.e., one product unit or one service deliverable) using this process?

Staffing: How many people do you employ or do you plan to employ? Break it down by full- and part-time staff, and what their roles and salary/wages are. Where do you get your staff (for example, from employment agencies, advertising, recruiting firms)?

Plan Write-Up: Weave your answers together into a paragraph, with bullet points when necessary.

C. EQUIPMENT, SUPPLIES AND PACKAGING

Equipment Needs: Give a brief overview of your equipment needs, and whether your process is minimal, moderate, or capital intensive. From where do you source your equipment, and do you rent, lease, or buy it? For each piece of specialized equipment, what does it do, why is it critical, how long will it last, and what is its capacity?

EQUIPMENT LIST

Equipment	Purpose	Capacity	Cost

Supplies: Give a brief overview of the raw materials or supplies that go into producing your product or delivering your service. Where do you source your raw materials and supplies? What are their lead times, minimum orders, and payment terms? What raw materials and supplies do you need to make your product?

SUPPLY LIST

Supply Item	Purpose	Capacity	Cost

Packaging: Describe your packaging. Is it a blister pack, shrink-wrapped box, or do you not require packaging? Explain why your packaging has been chosen, and how it reflects or differentiates your brand.

Plan Write-Up: Weave your answers together into a paragraph, with bullet points and subheadings when necessary.

D. ORDER FULFILLMENT, BILLING, AND CUSTOMER SERVICE

Fulfillment: Who fulfills your orders? Is this process done in-house or is it outsourced? Who's in charge? What are the steps involved to fill an order? Which of the following parts is automated, or could be automated?

1. Order Taking
2. Order Preparation (or pick-and-packing)
3. Shipping
4. Order Tracking

Billing: How are orders paid for? What is your billing method/process?

Customer Service: What is your customer service process or policy, and who is in charge of it? Discuss relevant warranties, guarantees, refunds, exchanges, credit assistance, etc.

Support: Do you provide any free or paid after-sales support? Discuss any maintenance, online, or phone support you provide.

Plan Write-Up: Weave your answers together into a paragraph, with bullet points and subheadings when necessary.

E. CONTROLS

Quality: How do you ensure product or service quality in your business? At what stages of the production process or service-delivery process does an outside person inspect quality? Be specific. Blanket statements like "staff checks their own quality" are meaningless, and serve no purpose. How often do you check the quality of your output? Periodically or daily? How do you motivate staff to do quality work? When and how do you solicit feedback from paying customers?

Inventory: Who is in charge of inventory management? What type of inventory-management system do you have in place? What is a safe level of inventory? Do you carry safety stock as a backup? Describe how you reorder raw materials or inventory stock. How long does it take to replenish your stock?

Compliance: What regulatory compliance procedures is your business subject to? If you have a preprinted list from a regulatory body, include it in an operations plan appendix.

Plan Write-Up: Weave your answers together into a paragraph, with bullet points and subheadings when necessary.

The key to an efficient operation is to focus on production or service-delivery steps that create value for the customer, and eliminate steps that don't. Process efficiency through automation will lower costs and improve quality. In this chapter, you provided the operations process behind your business plan to demonstrate that you are capable of operating your business and producing the product or delivering the service that you are promising. In the next chapter, the conclusion, we'll finalize the business plan creation process and discuss next steps.

Conclusion

The Dragons' Den Playbook

The Eight Sections of a Business Plan in Review and Next Steps

"There is a sure way to avoid criticism: be nothing and do nothing."
—Napoleon Hill[1]

THE DRAGONS' DEN PLAYBOOK

Draft the eight core sections of your business plan. Summarize your plan in a one- to two-page executive summary. Add supporting documents. Reformat your plan if a bank or an investor requests a specific format. Revise and refine your plan over time until you have a winning business strategy.

Max Factor found a market for his cosmetics in the movie industry, before he launched his own brand. Elizabeth Arden started selling her cosmetics line out of her first Red Door Salon in New York City. And Mary Kay started selling her cosmetics line through independent sales reps who were looking to open their own businesses. All of these famous entrepreneurs sold similar product lines, but followed radically different business plans to get their businesses off the ground. If you were part of their business-planning teams, you would have immediately noticed that not only were their product lines unique in terms of quality, but they also had completely different business models, sales and marketing strategies, and management structures. Every business is different, so every business plan must be unique. Create a business plan that works for you by testing and questioning your strategy until you find one that customers respond to.

THE DRAGONS' DEN PLAYBOOK: THE EIGHT SECTIONS OF A BUSINESS PLAN IN REVIEW

A business plan is a 10- to 25-page (or more) document that is requested by investors and banks when you ask them for investment capital. When you start approaching investors and banks, you'll find that they all have their own formats, so be prepared to reformat your plan upon request. But never forget that the goal of a business plan is to tell the story of how your business fills a market gap, and how your business will succeed. Therefore, regardless of the format requested, be sure to tell your story, and get your point across in the eight key sections. Let's recap the eight core sections of a business plan:

Section 1: VISION, MISSION, GOALS
State your vision for your business, including your business structure, mission statement, financial and non-financial objectives and milestones, and company history.

Section 2: PRODUCT/SERVICE DESCRIPTION
Describe what you are selling, how your product or service works, and why it is unique.

Section 3: MARKET DEFINITION
Describe the customers who will buy from you, the size of the market for your type of product or service, and the market share that you expect to achieve.

Section 4: COMPETITIVE ANALYSIS
Describe your competitors in the marketplace, and how you plan to position your product or service against them.

Section 5: BUSINESS MODEL
Describe how you plan to make money.

Section 6: SALES AND MARKETING STRATEGY
Describe where you plan to make your product or service available to customers, and how you plan to attract customers to those channels.

Section 7: MANAGEMENT AND ORGANIZATION

Describe your team and how you plan to structure your business entity.

Section 8: FINANCIAL PLAN

Describe how you plan to finance your venture and how you expect it to perform financially.

Summarize Your Business Plan

1. **Vision, Mission, Goals:** "Our vision is to be . . ."
2. **Product/Service Description:** "We sell . . . and it works by . . ."
3. **Market Definition:** "The market for our product is . . ."
4. **Competitive Analysis:** "The competitors in our market space are . . ."
5. **Business Model:** "We make money by . . ."
6. **Sales and Marketing Strategy:** "Our go-to-market strategy is . . ."
7. **Management and Organization:** "Our team consists of . . ."
8. **Financial Plan:** "Our financial projections for the next three to five years are . . ."

NEXT STEPS: REFINING YOUR BUSINESS MODEL

Once you have drafted your business plan using the questions in this book, and the plan format in the appendix, return to your business plan on an annual or quarterly basis to update it. A business plan should be treated as a snapshot of your business strategy at any point in time. It is not carved in stone, so update your business plan whenever there is a material change to your operation. That way, you will be ready to provide the document to anyone who asks, in case you suddenly need outside funding.

Now, if you find that your plan is not working at all, I invite you to read the companion guide to this book, *The Dragons' Den Guide to Assessing Your Business Concept.* When a plan is not meeting your financial goals, say, one to three years into your venture, there may be a major flaw in your business concept. In this case, use the companion guide just mentioned to revise and refine your business concept until you are satisfied that it will meet market needs and achieve your profitability goals.

If you have enjoyed this book or want to learn more, please visit the book's website, www.johnvyge.com.

Good luck!

Appendix

Company Name and Logo

BUSINESS PLAN

Contact Person:

Company Address:

Phone:

Fax:

Email:

Website:

Contact Information:

Date:

Business Plan Copy Number:

Legal Disclaimer: This is a business plan and does not imply an offering of securities. This document is confidential.

TABLE OF CONTENTS

    D. Proprietary Assets
    E. Product Lifecycle
    F. Product Roadmap

3. MARKET DEFINITION
    A. Market Opportunity
    B. Target-Market Profile
    C. Growth Strategy

4. COMPETITIVE ANALYSIS
    A. Competition
    B. Competitive Advantage
    C. Barriers to Entry

5. BUSINESS MODEL
    A. Value Chain
    B. Product/Market Fit
    C. Revenue Model
    D. Scalability

6. SALES AND MARKETING STRATEGY
    A. Positioning
    B. Pricing Strategy
    C. Sales Strategy
    D. Marketing Strategy
    E. Strategic Relationships
    F. Sales Forecast

7. MANAGEMENT AND ORGANIZATION
    A. Business Organization
    B. Management Team
    C. Advisory Board
    D. Professional Support
    E. Hiring Needs

8. FINANCIAL PLAN
    A. Financial Summary
    B. Financing Details

C. Financial Performance
D. Risk and Mitigation

SUPPORTING DOCUMENTS
- Management Resumés
- Legal Documents
- Product or Service Diagrams and Flow Charts
- Personal Financial Statements
- Operations Plan

EXECUTIVE SUMMARY

- What is the name of your company, what does your business do, when did you start, and what is the most amazing thing about your business concept?
- What problem does your product or service solve?
- What is your core product or service, how does it work, and why is it valuable?
- How do you plan to make money?
- What is the size of the market for your product or service?
- Who are your competitors and what is the sustainable advantage you have over them?
- Who are your potential customers?
- Who is on your team and what domain expertise and deep market experience uniquely qualify them to execute the plan?
- Who are your customers? How do you plan to get customers? What strategic partners can help you go to market faster?
- What financial, technical, or market milestones have you reached that prove that your concept will work?

FINANCIAL SUMMARY

	Year 1	Year 2	Year 3	Year 4	Year 5
Revenue					
Cost of Goods					
Gross Margin					
Operating Expenses*					
EBITDA					

*excluding depreciation and amortization

- How much capital do you need? What are you willing to give up? What will you use the funds for?
- What options do you (or the potential investor) have for an exit in the future? Who could potentially acquire your business?

1. VISION, MISSION, GOALS

A. Business Description

- What is the name of your company, and how long have you been in business?
- What type of legal entity have you established, and how many owners are there?
- What product or service do you sell?
- Who will buy/use your product or service?
- How will you generate repeat revenues annually? Will you produce and market your products yourself, or license them to others who pay you a transaction fee?

B. Vision and Mission

- What will your business look like in three to five years? In what business category and geographic market will you be the leader?
- What is the highest and best use for your product or service? What problem does it solve? How does it improve people's lives? How does it help people?
- What will be your primary target market?
- What capability makes your team uniquely qualified to solve this problem?

C. Business Objectives

- What are your revenue, profit, and return on investment goals for the next three to five years?
- What are your non-financial business goals for the next three to five years (such as company size, location, new product lines)?

D. Milestones

- What milestones will you achieve in the near future?
- What major marketing, product-development, or operational projects are you looking to complete in the next six months to three years?

Major Projects Pending	Completion Date	Funding Required

E. Business History

- How far along are you with your business? What stage of development are you in? Do you have a prototype, or is your concept just notes on a napkin? Why are you writing this business plan, and why do you really need the funding?
- Why did you start the company? What prompted you to give up your day job and take a risk as an entrepreneur?

2. PRODUCT/SERVICE DESCRIPTION

A. Customer Problem

- What is the overriding customer problem that you are solving?

B. Product/Service Description

- Describe your product.
- How does it work?
- Where will your product be consumed or service performed?
- What types of products or services currently compete with yours?

C. Core Features and Benefits

- Finish this sentence: "Our product/service is the only one that . . ."
- What are two to three unique components of your product or service offering, and why are they important?
- How is your product or service faster, more convenient, or higher performing than alternative offerings on the market?
- What is the rational value (functional or monetary benefit) of your product or service? What is the emotional value of your product or service? What social value does your product or service provide?

- After the customer buys from you, what type of ongoing support do you provide for your product or service?

D. Proprietary Assets

- What are the proprietary features of your product or service (trademarks, patents, copyrights, licensing agreements, etc.)?

E. Product Lifecycle

- What stage of the lifecycle is your product or service in?

F. Product Roadmap

- What features will you roll out over time?
- What related products or services could you launch in the future?

3. MARKET DEFINITION

A. Market Opportunity

- Why does the market need a product or service like yours?
- What industry are you operating in? What is the total market size for your type of product or service in the geographic market space you will compete in? What is the compound annual growth rate of your industry?
- What drives demand in your industry? Is it product design, low price, a service option, or some other basis for competition?
- Who are the two or three major players in your industry?
- What industry trends support your business opportunity?
- How sensitive is your industry to the changing of the business cycle and/or the changing of the seasons?

B. Target-Market Profile

- What are your top three target markets?
- What rational motive will customers in your target markets have for buying your product/service, and how will your product/service meet this need? For example, *Our plumbing product plugs water leaks.*

- What emotional motive will your customers have for buying your product/service, and how will your product/service meet this need? For example, *Our security feature gives the customer peace of mind.*
- What social motives will your customers have for buying your product/service, and how will your product/service meet this need? For example, *We only use suppliers that adhere to fair-trade practices.*
- What productivity motives will your customers have for buying your product/service, and how will your product/service meet this need? For example, *Our rice maker helps chefs cook twice the rice in half the time.*
- What economic motives will your customers have for buying your product/service, and how will your product/service meet this need? For example, *Our leak sensor helps our customers cut down on their electricity bills by identifying air conditioner problems.*

C. Growth Strategy

- What is your growth strategy (for example, acquisition, merger, new markets, new products)?
- How will you increase your current market's usage of your product or service on a per-customer basis?
- What new applications might there be for your product or service that would appeal to new markets?
- What new markets will you target in the future?
- What new products could you upsell to your current customers in the future?

4. COMPETITIVE ANALYSIS

A. Competition

- Describe the competitive landscape of your product or service category.
- What is the basis for competition in your industry? (For example, product design, cost, service, etc.)
- Who are your three to five direct competitors? These are businesses that sell similar solutions to your type of product or service. (Don't limit your description to businesses within your geographic region.) What are their relevant strengths and weaknesses?

DIRECT COMPETITORS

Competitor	Strengths	Weaknesses

Who are your three to five indirect competitors? These are the companies that sell products or services that are different than yours, but that solve the same problem. For example, tax-preparation software vs. a tax-preparation service, or tea vs. coffee. (Don't limit your description to businesses within your geographic region.) What are their relevant strengths and weaknesses?

INDIRECT COMPETITORS

Competitor	Strengths	Weaknesses

B. Competitive Advantage
- Why would someone choose your product or service over that of your competition?
- What is your competitive advantage, and why is it sustainable? Do you have a cost, feature, or service advantage over your competitors?

C. Barriers to Entry
- What hurdles would new market entrants have to overcome to compete with you?
- What barriers to entry make it difficult for new competitors to enter the market? (For example, start-up costs, regulatory barriers such as time-consuming or expensive licensing requirements, intellectual-property acquisition costs, etc.)

5. BUSINESS MODEL

A. Value Chain
- Identify the two to three key players in your industry. Describe the traditional links in the value chain of your product or service category. Be specific about who adds value and how. Discuss how your value chain is similar to or different from the traditional model.
- Who are the major players in your industry?
- Who conceives of and designs the product that the major players sell?
- How is your product or service produced?
- Who establishes the relationships with the outlets that make the product or service physically available to the ultimate consumer? For example, are their distributors or agents who can market your product to retailers on your behalf?
- Who transports the product to the outlet that sells it?
- Who makes the product or service physically available to the ultimate consumer?

B. Product/Market Fit
- Make a list of every potential customer who could pay you for your product or service. Explain why they would pay you, and describe how you would get paid.
- For each revenue stream and customer served, name the product or service that could be sold to that person, business entity, or organization.

C. Revenue Model
- What is your revenue model? Why did you choose it? Why will it be effective? If you have a different revenue model for each product you sell or customer you serve, mention that in this section.

D. Scalability
- Why is your business model scalable? Specifically, how is your business set up to handle varying levels of sales volume?

6. SALES AND MARKETING STRATEGY
- What will be the key to your sales and marketing success? What primary channel will you use, and what market share will you capture?
- What are your sales objectives? What are your marketing objectives?

A. Positioning

- What product or service category are you competing in?
- What is your unique selling proposition in the markets you will compete in? Specifically, what feature, process, problem-solving attribute, benefit, or other fact about your product or service is currently your main selling point?
- What secondary benefits of your product stand out the most?
- What target market group in particular will be most responsive to this positioning?

B. Pricing Strategy

- What is your overall pricing objective? Are you looking for short-term profit, to match competitor prices, to build market share, or to establish a perception of high quality? Do you have a low-price, high-volume strategy, or a high-price, low-volume strategy?
- How do you calculate your price(s) (i.e. cost-based, market-based, competition-based)? If you have several products, list them and describe the pricing methodology for each.
- Will you be offering any periodic discounts to consumers? If you are selling through intermediaries, what volume deals, bonus units, allowances, or co-op contributions will you be making?
- How do you justify your prices, and how does your marketing strategy help you achieve your sales (or revenue) and marketing objectives?
- How does your price level reflect your brand image? What is your price level compared to your competition?
- Discuss the sensitivity of your target market to pricing, and how you will track and respond to the price sensitivity of your customers.
- What is the lowest price you could charge and still generate a profit?
- What is the highest price you could charge and still have customers willing to pay you?
- What price point(s) will generate the highest number of customers?

C. Sales Strategy

- What is your sales strategy?
- Describe your sales strategy in two to three sentences, and explain why it is the most effective way to sell your product or service. Discuss the sales channels (and specific stores/distributors/agents where applicable) that you already have in place, those you are

planning for in the future, and how much each channel will contribute as a percentage of overall sales.

- How long is the sales cycle? In other words, how long does it take, on average, from the time you first make contact with a prospective customer to the time the customer places an order?
- How will your customers pay for your products or services? Are there any payment terms?
- What type of sales incentives will you offer and why?
- What type of discount pricing will you offer and why?
- What is your sales strategy?
- What is your rollout strategy?

ROLLOUT STRATEGY

Sales Channel	Specific Outlets	Date

D. Marketing Strategy

- In two to three sentences, describe your marketing communications strategy. What will be the most effective tool for building awareness of your brand? Will you be targeting businesses, intermediaries, or end-users?
- What is your communications budget as a percentage of projected revenue?
- What are your communications objectives? (For example, mass reach or niche penetration.)
- What specific media outlets attract your target audience? (For example, print, online, or social media) Can you identify by name some publications that reach your customers?
- What publicity tools will you use to attract customers?
- Who will refer business to you and why?
- What trade shows attract your target audience?
- What are your marketing methods?

MARKETING METHODS

Marketing Tactic	Description	Budget

E. Strategic Relationships

- What strategic relationships have you established or will you establish in the future?
- What other product or service would you be willing to co-brand yours with?
- What type of manufacturer could license your product (or service model)?
- Do you have a business model that lends itself to franchising?
- Are there any markets that you cannot enter without partnering with another business? If so, what specific businesses would you be willing to establish a joint venture with?
- What types of products or services complement yours? What types of products or services would bundle your product with theirs as part of their offering?
- What are your plans for establishing strategic relationships?

STRATEGIC RELATIONSHIPS

Partner	Description	Budget

F. Sales Forecast

- Choose a sales forecasting method that best fits your product/market focus. Then build your sales forecast.

SALES PROJECTION BY PRODUCT TYPE

Product/Service	Year 1	Year 2	Year 3	Year 4	Year 5
1					
2					
3					
4					
Total Sales Projection					

PROJECTED SALES BY MARKET SEGMENT

Market Segment	Year 1	Year 2	Year 3	Year 4	Year 5
1					
2					
3					
4					
Total Sales Projection					

PROJECTED SALES BY FEES CHARGED TO CUSTOMERS

Fees Charged	Year 1	Year 2	Year 3	Year 4	Year 5
1					
2					
3					
4					
Total Sales Projection					

7. MANAGEMENT AND ORGANIZATION

- What is your human resources strategy?
- Where do you find your talent pool?
- What training is required for people to work for you?

- What is the culture of your business? What values are important to you in your work? Is it a formal or informal working environment? Describe it.

A. Business Organization

- Where is your business located?
- What type of entity is your business?
- How is your ownership currently structured? Who owns your business and in what percentages?
- What types of licenses and permits have you secured or do you need to secure?

B. Management Team

- Who is responsible for running your business, and what is their job title?
- Who is responsible for sales and marketing, and what is their job title?
- Who is responsible for finance, and what is their job title?
- In this section of your business plan, list the key personnel who will be on your management team, their titles, and what relevant backgrounds and expertise they bring to the table.

C. Advisory Board

- In what areas of your business (finance, marketing, strategy) will you require unpaid third-party advice from time to time?
- Who in your circle of influence works, or has worked, in marketing who would be willing to serve on your advisory board? Make sure they don't currently work for one of your competitors.
- Who do you know who works, or has worked, in finance who would be willing to serve on your advisory board?
- Who do you know who owns a successful business who would be willing to serve on your advisory board?
- Make contact with those people who might serve on your advisory board, and ask them if they would be willing to serve.
- In this section of your business plan, list the four to five people who have agreed to serve on your advisory board, and outline the relevant experience and expertise that they bring to the table.

D. Professional Support
- Who will help you with bookkeeping or tax advice?
- Who will provide you with legal advice?
- Who will provide you with business insurance?
- In this section of your business plan, summarize the professional support that you can access on an as-needed basis.

E. Hiring Needs
- How many employees will you need to run your business?
- What is the total payroll that you will require to meet your objectives in the first three years of business?

HUMAN RESOURCES PLAN

Employee Information	Year 1	Year 2	Year 3
Number of Employees			
Management Salaries			
Staff Wages			
Total Payroll			

8. FINANCIAL PLAN

A. Overview
- What are the highlights of your financial plan?
- What revenue do you expect to achieve in Years 1, 2, and 3?
- How many units of your product or service do you need to sell to break even on a monthly basis?
- How long will it take to recoup or pay back your initial investment?
- When will your business turn a profit?
- In order to achieve your profit targets, what assumptions have you made with respect to cost of goods sold, operating expenses, interest, tax, supplier terms, etc.?
- What amount of capital are you seeking?

FINANCIAL OVERVIEW

Financial Metric	Year 1	Year 2	Year 3	Year 4	Year 5
Revenue					
Cost of Goods					
Gross Margin					
Operating Expenses*					
EBITDA					

*excluding interest, tax, depreciation & amortization

B. Financing Details

- How much capital are you requesting from investors?
- How will you use the capital?

CAPITALIZATION TABLE

Investor	Date	Investment	Shares	Ownership
Common				
Preferred				
Totals				100%

- How will the investor get his or her money back? In this section, mention potential acquirers, a share buy-back, royalty, merger, or other liquidity event that could cash out the investor in the future.

C. Financial Performance

- Create an income statement that shows your projected income, expenses, and profit for the next three to five years.

INCOME STATEMENT (OR P&L STATEMENT)

	Year 1	Year 2	Year 3	Year 4	Year 5
REVENUE					
Sales (A)					
Direct Labour Cost (B)					
Direct Material Cost (C)					
COGS	= B + C				
Gross Profit (D)	D = A - (B + C)				
Less: EXPENSES					
Advertising & Promotion					
Car & Truck Expenses					
Commission & Fees					
Contract Labour					
Depreciation & Amortization					
Employee Benefits					
Insurance					
Legal & Professional Fees					
Office Expenses					
Rent or Lease					
Repairs & Maintenance					
Supplies					
Licenses & Permits					
Travel, Meals, & Entertainment					
Utilities					
Salaries & Wages*					
Other Expenses (i.e. Storage, Freight, etc.)					
Total Expenses (E)					
Net Income from Operations	= D- E				
Less: Interest Expense					

(Continued)

Net Income Before Taxes					
Less: Tax Expense					
Net Income/Loss					

*Selling, general and administrative salaries and wages. Any wages paid to make the product are included in the cost of goods sold (COGS) section.

- Create a balance sheet that shows the projected assets, debts, and owners' equity in your business for one year (or for the next three to five years, if assets and liabilities are significant).

BALANCE SHEET

	Year 1	Year 2	Year 3	Year 4	Year 5
ASSETS					
Current Assets					
Cash					
Accounts Receivable					
Inventory					
Prepaid Expenses					
Total Current Assets					
Fixed Assets					
Land					
Buildings					
Depreciation Offset					
Equipment					
Depreciation Offset					
Furniture & Fixtures					
Autos & Vehicles					
Other Assets					
Total Fixed Assets					
TOTAL ASSETS					

	Year 1	Year 2	Year 3	Year 4	Year 5
LIABILITIES					
Current Liabilities					
Accounts Payable					
Short-Term Debt					
Accrued Liabilities					
Other Current Liabilities					
Total Current Liabilities					
Long-Term Liabilities					
Long-Term Debt					
Other Liabilities					
Total Long-Term Liabilities					
EQUITY					
Owners' Investment					
Retained Earnings					
Total Equity					
TOTAL LIABILITIES & EQUITY					

- Create a cash-flow statement that shows your projected cash receipts, disbursements, and net cash flow for the next 12 months (or for the next three to five years, if your cash flows differ significantly from your income statement).

MONTHLY CASH-FLOW STATEMENT

	1	2	3	4	5	6	7	8	9	10	11	12
Cash Inflows												
Cash Sales												
Receivables Paid												
Loan Proceeds												

(*Continued*)

	1	2	3	4	5	6	7	8	9	10	11	12
Invested Capital												
Other Cash Receipts												
Total Cash Inflows												
Cash Outflows												
Cash COGS												
Cash Operating Expenses												
Cash Purchases												
Loan Payments												
Investor Payback												
Owners' Draw												
Taxes Paid												
Other Disbursements												
Total Cash Outflows												
Net Cash Flow												

- Using the income statement and balance sheet, calculate the ratios for your business using the formulas explained in Chapter 18.

RATIO ANALYSIS

	Year 1	Year 2	Year 3	Year 4	Year 5
Profitability					
Net Profit Margin					
Return on Investment					
Return on Equity					
Liquidity					
Current Ratio					
Quick Ratio					
Inventory Turnover Ratio					

	Year 1	Year 2	Year 3	Year 4	Year 5
Debt					
Debt-to-Equity					
Time Interest Earned					

D. Risk and Mitigation

- What liability risks does your business face? Why would someone sue you?
- What market risks does your business face? What market factor or new competitor could put you out of business?
- What regulatory risks does your business face? What current or new regulations could hinder your ability to do business?
- What operating risks does your business face? What supply or staffing shortages could hurt your business?
- What financial risks does your business face?
- What other risks does your business face?
- What steps are you taking to mitigate these risks? (For example, insurance, patents, HR policies, terms of trade, etc.)

SUPPORTING DOCUMENTS

- Manager bios or resumés
- Legal documents (patents, intellectual property, contracts, distribution agreements, etc.)
- Product or service diagrams or flow charts
- Personal financial statements (upon request)
- Operations plan (upon request)

GLOSSARY

Advisory Board A group of paid or unpaid industry experts or skilled people that you set up to mentor you.

Angel Investor A high-net-worth individual who actively invests in businesses.

Barrier to Entry A regulatory, legal, intellectual property, or time hurdle that would prevent a competitor from copying your business model or its products and services.

Basis for Competition How the majority of competitors in your market currently compete for customers.

Behavioural Profile A description of a target market based on its activities, lifestyles, hobbies, etc.

Bootstrap Investing your own money in your business to get the business off the ground.

Bottom-Up Approach Learning about your market by conducting primary research with businesses in your industry to estimate the number of potential customers in your geographic market who may use your category of product or service.

Business Description An explanation in your business plan of what your business does.

Business History A part in your business plan where you describe what inspired your business idea in the first place, and what you have achieved to date.

Business Model A strategy for making money that takes into consideration the product or service sold, customers served, and revenue model used.

Business Objectives A part in your business plan where you describe your financial and non-financial goals.

Buying Motive The event, trigger, or need that causes someone to buy from you.

Call to Action Making a specific request to an investor for funding, a second meeting, or an introduction to a third party.

Capacity The order volume that you are prepared to fill given your current operational setup.

Capital Intensive A business that requires more equipment and technology to produce its product than it does labour. For example, a widget manufacturer.

Channel An outlet through which products and services are made available for sale.

COGS *See* Cost of Goods Sold (COGS).

Competitive Advantage An edge that you have in the marketplace over your competitors, such as cost, features, or a service component.

Competitor Any alternative business or method that a customer currently uses to solve a problem or meet a need.

Copyright An exclusive legal right to your drawings, software, books, articles, music, or other works. Holding a copyright prevents others from copying your original work. Speak to a lawyer to clarify your rights and options.

Corporation A stand-alone entity where the shareholders are not responsible for the debts or liabilities of the business.

Cost of Goods Sold (COGS) The cost of direct materials and labour to produce your inventory, or the direct cost of the finished product that you market.

Customer Service Providing support to customers while they buy, use, maintain, or return your product (or service).

Deal An agreement between an investor and a company, where the investor gives capital in exchange for equity or convertible debt in the business.

Deal Flow The number of deals that investors receive for review over a certain period of time.

Deal Killer Something that the investor uncovers during the due diligence process that causes him or her to pull out of a tentative deal to fund your business.

Demographic Profile A description of your ideal target market based on its average age, income, education, and occupation.

Due Diligence A process of reviewing your financial, operational, and legal history to make sure that your business plan doesn't have any false or misleading assumptions or expectations.

Earnings Multiple Valuation Method Average net profit of your business times x, where x is a multiple based on sales of similar businesses.

EBITDA Earnings before interest, taxes, depreciation, and amortization. An indicator of how well the business operation is running, irrespective of the financing methods used.

Elevator Pitch A brief verbal presentation to an investor that describes your business model and calls the investor to action.

Equity You're Giving Up The percentage of your company you give to the investor in return for his or her investment.

Executive Summary A one- to two-page summary of the highlights of your business plan, in text, with diagrams.

Exit Strategy How an investor or founding entrepreneur will get his or her investment out of the business, such as by a third-party acquisition of the business.

Financial Due Diligence A review of your business and personal financial background to make sure that you can live up to all the promises you made to investors with respect to revenues and expenses, and assets and liabilities.

Financial Investor An individual who agrees to provide capital, introductions to future investors, and negotiation expertise to your business.

Flow Chart A one-page diagram that shows the core stages in your operational processes.

Fulfillment The process of filling an order that has been placed with your business.

Fundable Business Concept Another word for investable business concept.

Funding The investment capital you receive to grow your business.

Fundraising The investor-courting process.

Geographic Profile A description of a target market based on its location, such as country, region, province, or city.

Gross Profit Revenue less your cost of goods sold.

Hiring Needs The additional staff that you will need to hire to run your business.

Income Statement A statement of revenues, expenses, and net profit, also known as a profit and loss statement, or P&L.

Industry Sector The companies that operate selling similar services or products.

Initial Public Offering (IPO) When shares are listed on the stock exchange and traded publicly.

Introduction When someone who vouches for your credibility refers you to an investor.

Investable Business Concept A business concept that meets the return on investment expectations and industry or other preferences of investors.

Investor Pipeline The number of investors you are introduced to over a certain period of time.

IPO *See* Initial Public Offering (IPO).

Labour Intensive A business that requires more labour to produce its product than it does equipment and technology. For example, a landscaping business.

Legal Due Diligence A review of your legal position in critical areas such as contracts, intellectual property, or outstanding legal judgments.

Liquidity Event An exit strategy for an investor that enables the investor or founding entrepreneur to convert some or all of his or her shares into cash.

Manager Someone who is in charge of a specific business function, such as sales, marketing, operations, finance, or technology.

Market Segment A homogeneous group of customers who are similar in some way, such as geographic, demographic, psychographic, or behavioural characteristics.

Market Size The total sales volume of the products or services sold in a specific geographic market.

Marketing The process of attracting attention to your product or service.

Metaphor Something that is representative or symbolic of your product or service that will give it context in a business plan. For example, "Our wearable multimedia player is a mini TV set that you wear on your shirt."

Mezzanine Financing A round of funding that comes just before an IPO.

Milestone A measurable achievement that you expect to reach if you receive funding from an investor. In a business plan, you should outline the milestones you expect to complete by certain deadlines.

Mission A statement of how your business helps your customers. A mission statement should be included in a business plan.

Monetize To convert a product or service into a revenue-generating asset.

Niche A product that you plan to sell, and a clearly defined market that you plan to sell it to. Also known as a product/market fit.

Net Profit What's left over after all costs of goods sold, operating expenses, interest expenses, and taxes have been paid.

Non-compete Agreement An agreement that gives you the right to prevent employees from leaving and setting up shop in the same business you are in. Speak to a lawyer to clarify your rights and options.

Non-disclosure Agreement (NDA) An agreement not to share confidential information with others.

Offshoring Using a business in another country to execute all or part of your processes.

Operating Expenses The selling, general, and administrative expenses that you incur to sell your products and services (for example, sales commissions or travel costs) and administer your business (for example, rent, utilities, office salaries, office supplies, insurance, licenses, etc.).

Operational Due Diligence A review of your operational processes to make sure that your business is capable of doing what you say it is capable of doing.

Organizational Chart An organizational chart uses boxes and lines to show the management structure of a business and relevant reporting lines.

Outsourcing Paying another business to execute all or part of your processes.

P&L *See* Profit and Loss Statement (P&L).

Partnership A multi-person business where the general partners are 100% liable for all debts of the business.

Patent The exclusive right to the creation and sale of your invention or internal processes. Obtaining a patent prevents others from copying and selling your work. Speak to a lawyer to clarify your rights and options.

Payback Period The amount of time it takes for the investor to earn their capital back.

Pitch A verbal, visual, or written presentation to an investor or investor group that describes how your business makes money, and explains why the investor should invest.

Post-money Valuation The value of your business after the investor's capital is injected into it.

Pre-money Valuation The value of your business before the investor's capital is injected into it.

Pre-screening An initial evaluation of your business that is undertaken by the investor to weed out proposals are not compatible with his or her own personal investing criteria (such as industry sector, market, or geographic region).

Product Lifecycle The sales cycle that your product or service category goes through, from introduction, growth, maturity, and decline stages.

Product Roadmap A feature-development schedule for your product or service.

Product/Market Fit A product or service that has a market large enough to meet your financial and non-financial objectives. Also known as a niche.

Professional Support Paid outside consultants who provide tax, legal, marketing, or other advice.

Profit and Loss Statement (P&L) A statement of revenues and expenses, also known as an income statement.

Proprietary Assets Features or intellectual-property assets that are protected from competitors through trade secrets or intellectual-property protection rights.

Psychographic Profile A description of a target market based on its personality traits.

Return on Investment (ROI) The investor's required rate of return.

Revenue Model How you charge for your products or services.

Revenue Multiple Valuation Method Revenue times y, where y is a multiple based on sales of similar businesses.

ROI *See* Return on Investment (ROI).

Rollout Strategy How you plan to add new sales channels and penetrate new markets over time.

Round (or Funding Round) A layer of investment capital that is provided to your business to get you to a specific milestone in your business.

Sales The process of pushing your products and services out to customers through various channels.

Sales Cycle The length of time between your first contact with a prospective customer and the point at which the customer places an order.

Scalability The ability of a business to handle a sudden increase in customer volume without being constrained by staff or financial limitations.

Screening An evaluation of your business concept against a standard set of factors to see if it meets certain criteria that are set by an investor.

Sector A portion of a market that you are targeting with your business concept.

Seed Stage The earliest stage of a business, when you're trying to prove that you have a viable business idea. Seed capital is the money provided by the investor at this stage.

Series A The first round of funding provided by a venture capital firm. Subsequent letters refer to subsequent injections of capital.

Self-Audit Review your business to make sure that it meets certain criteria that investors will look for.

Slide Presentation A PowerPoint presentation that explains your business concept visually to an investor in 10 to 15 slides.

Sole Proprietorship A single-person business where the owner is 100% liable for all debts of the business.

Strategic Investors Provide sector or business-model experience to your business, in addition to providing financial capital.

Strategic Relationship An arm's-length relationship between two or more parties to achieve a shared objective.

Strategic Value Contacts, industry experience, and expertise that an investor can give you in addition to financial capital.

Top-Down Approach Researching the total industry-wide sales volume of a product or service type so that a market-share percentage can be used to project your sales.

Trade Secrets Confidential internal processes or formulas that you don't want shared with the public and other competitors. Speak to a lawyer about how to protect trade secrets.

Trademark Legally registered words or symbols that companies use to differentiate their products from others. A trademark prevents others from copying your business name, logo, and symbols. Speak to a lawyer to clarify your rights and options.

Traditional Business Model The most commonly found business models including retail, franchise, or direct sales.

Triple Bottom Line Business (Also known as people, profit, and planet.) A business that sets out to achieve business profit while acting in a socially responsible (people) and environmentally friendly manner (planet).

Upsell Selling an add-on or adding more unit volume to a purchase that a customer has agreed to make. For example, "Would you like fries with that?" or "Would you like a three-year extended warranty with that?"

Valuation The dollar value of your business as estimated by you or an investor.

Value Chain The entities through which your product or service passes before it reaches the final customer—with each entity adding value along the way.

Value Proposition A declarative statement of why the world is better off with your product or service than without it.

Venture Capital Investment capital that comes from investors who invest other investors' money in businesses like yours.

Vision What you want your business to look like or be the leader of in the future.

"Wow" Factor Something about your product or service that has never been seen before, or that makes it compelling to buy.

Notes

CHAPTER 3. DO YOU HAVE A FUNDABLE BUSINESS CONCEPT?

1. Eric Wilson, "Liz Claiborne, Designer, Dies at 78," *New York Times*, June 27, 2007, http://www.nytimes.com/2007/06/27/fashion/27cnd-claiborne.html?pagewanted=all.

CHAPTER 4. HOW MUCH CAPITAL WILL YOU NEED?

1. E. Scott Beattie, letter to shareholders, *Elizabeth Arden Annual Report 2010*, 4.
2. "About Elizabeth Arden," Elizabeth Arden Inc., accessed July 3, 2012, http://corporate.elizabetharden.com/about-elizabeth-arden.php.

CHAPTER 6. PITCHING TO INVESTORS

1. "About Us," Piggly Wiggly official website, accessed July 14, 2012, http://www.pigglywiggly.com/about-us.

CHAPTER 7. ELEVATOR PITCH

1. Carl von Clausewitz, *On War* (New York: Penguin Books, 1982).

CHAPTER 8. EXECUTIVE SUMMARY

1. Darren Rovell, "Tough Mudder Brings In $25 Million, Signs Under Armour," CNBC.com, December 5, 2011, http://www.cnbc.com/id/45554832/Tough_Mudder_Brings_In_25_Million_Signs_Under_Armour.

CHAPTER 9. INVESTOR PRESENTATION

1. Lee Gomes, "PowerPoint Turns 20, As Its Creators Ponder a Dark Side to Success," *Wall Street Journal*, June 20, 2007, http://online.wsj.com/article/SB118228116940840904.html.

CHAPTER 11. WHAT IS YOUR VISION FOR YOUR BUSINESS?

1. "Company: Company Founder," Mary Kay Inc. official website, accessed June 12, 2012, http://www.marykay.com/company/companyfounder/default.aspx.
2. http://media.ethicalocean.com/pressbioth.html. Last accessed August 5th, 2012.
3. Ibid.

CHAPTER 16. HOW WILL YOU GET CUSTOMERS?

1. "Company History," L.L. Bean Inc. official website, accessed June 21, 2012, http://www.llbean.com/customerService/aboutLLBean/company_history.html.

CHAPTER 18. HOW WILL YOU FUND YOUR PLAN?

1. United States Patent Office, Patent No. 306,727, October 21, 1884.
2. http://www4.agr.gc.ca/AAFC-AAC/display-afficher.do?id=1171305207040 Last accessed August 7, 2012

CONCLUSION. THE DRAGONS' DEN PLAYBOOK

1. Napoleon Hill, *The Law of Success in Sixteen Lessons* (New York: Jeremy P. Tarcher, 1928), 438.

About the Author

John Vyge is a Certified Financial Planner™ professional and business plan analyst who advises entrepreneurs and investors on how to create investor-ready business plans around winning business concepts. He researches fast-growth companies to develop insight for his recommendations. John is the author of *The Dragons' Den Guide to Assessing Your Business Concept* and *Model Marketing Kit*, a contributing author for *Investing in an Uncertain Economy for Dummies*, and a technical reviewer for *76 Tips for Investing in an Uncertain Economy for Canadians for Dummies*. He has been quoted in various publications including *The Washington Post*, *Business Week* online, *Investment News Magazine*, BankRate.com, and *Insurance & Advisor* magazine.

ACKNOWLEDGEMENTS

Thank you for buying this book, because the real catalyst for this book is you—an entrepreneur who has decided to take action on a business idea, with the hope of changing your life for the better. Everyone who watches *Dragons' Den* loves it—not just because it's entertaining, but because it shows every person in this country that an idea can be turned into a business that will change their life and the community around them.

There are many people who need to be thanked for putting this book together:

The team at CBC *Dragons' Den*, including Marc Thompson, Tracie Tighe, and Karen Bower, with specific thanks to Molly Duignan, producer of CBC *Dragons' Den* and resident expert on the show, and to Dianne Buckner, host of *Dragons' Den*, for contributing the foreword. Thanks also go to Lisa O'Connell and Lindsay Pearl at Sony/2WayTraffic for making the project possible.

The team at Wiley, with a special call-out to Jeremy Hanson-Finger, production editor, and Jane Withey, developmental editor, as well as the copyeditor, Jackie Lee.

Several others who also need to be thanked include James Murphy, a personal development expert and executive coach at Evolution for Success, who added insight and technical value to the Self-Assessment section of this book, as well as Luc Hekman, Jean-Marc Poirier, Raj Ananthanpillai, David Lester, Brien Fraser, Lars Bodenheimer, and Raj Narasimhan, who provided support through the writing process.

Personal thanks go to my wife's cousin, author Marilyn Picard, for connecting me to Wiley; my entrepreneurial father-in-law, John Milne, Sr.; my mother-in-law, for her constant support and quiet strength; and my parents John and Annette Vyge, for their support and inspiration. And, finally, my wife and partner in life, Sandy, for her support, and our two children, Trinity and Whitney, who helped me think through many of the words on these pages during our routine "monster walks" through the parks and fields around our home. Your passion for learning new things continues to inspire me every day.

INDEX

Looking for More?

VISIT WWW.JOHNVYGE.COM

Talk to the author online
Share your brand story
Download worksheets
and more . . .

Bring these concepts into your business through training initiatives,
consulting engagements, and keynote addresses.